The Digital Handshake: Connecting Internet Bac...

Table of Contents

Table of Figures

The Digital Handshake: Connecting Internet Backbones

Executive Summary

This paper examines the interconnection arrangements that enable Internet users to communicate with one another from computers that are next door or on the other side of the globe. The Internet is a network of networks, owned and operated by different companies, including Internet backbone providers. In order to provide end users with universal connectivity, Internet backbones must interconnect with one another to exchange traffic destined for each other's end users. Internet backbone providers are not governed by any industry-specific interconnection regulations, unlike other providers of network services; instead, each backbone provider bases its decisions on whether, how, and where to interconnect by weighing the benefits and costs of each interconnection. Interconnection agreements between Internet backbone providers are reached through commercial negotiations in a "handshake" environment. Internet backbones interconnect under two different arrangements: peering or transit. In a peering arrangement, backbones agree to exchange traffic with each other at no cost. The backbones only exchange traffic that is destined for each other's end users, not the end users of a third party. In a transit arrangement, on the other hand, one backbone pays another backbone for interconnection. In exchange for this payment, the transit supplier provides a connection to all end users on the Internet.

The interconnection policies that have evolved in place of industry-specific regulations are examined here, in order to determine the impact of these policies on the markets for Internet services. In the past several years, a number of parties in the United States and abroad have questioned whether larger backbone providers are able to gain or exploit market power through the terms of interconnection that they offer to smaller existing and new backbone providers. In the future, backbones may attempt to differentiate themselves by offering certain new services only to their own customers. As a result, the concern is that the Internet may "balkanize," with competing backbones not interconnecting to provide all services. This paper demonstrates how, in the absence of a dominant backbone, market forces encourage interconnection between backbones and thereby protect consumers from any anti-competitive behavior on the part of backbone providers. While it is likely that market forces, in combination with antitrust and competition policy, can guarantee that no dominant backbone emerges, if a dominant backbone provider should emerge through unforeseen circumstance, regulation may be necessary, as it has been in other network industries such as telephony.

The paper also examines an international interconnection issue. In recent years, some carriers, particularly those from the Asia-Pacific region, have claimed that it is unfair that they must pay for the whole cost of the transmission capacity between international points and the United States that is used to carry Internet traffic between these regions. After analyzing the case presented by these carriers, the paper concludes that the solution proposed by these carriers, legacy international telecommunications regulations, should not be imposed on the Internet. To date, there is no evidence that the interconnection agreements between international carriers result from anti-competitive actions on the part of any backbones; therefore, the market for Internet backbone services is best governed by commercial interactions between private participants.

1

I. Introduction

The Internet is not a monolithic, uniform network; rather, it is a network of networks, owned and operated by different companies, including Internet backbone providers. Internet backbones deliver data traffic to and from their customers; often this traffic comes from, or travels to, customers of another backbone. Currently, there are no domestic or international industry-specific regulations that govern how Internet backbone providers interconnect to exchange traffic, unlike other network services, such as long distance voice services, for which interconnection is regulated.[1] Rather, Internet backbone providers adopt and pursue their own interconnection policies, governed only by ordinary laws of contract and property, overseen by antitrust rules. This paper examines the interconnection policies between Internet backbone providers that have evolved in place of industry-specific regulations, in order to examine the impact of these policies on the markets for Internet services.

The paper first examines the current system of interconnection, and then examines several recent developments. In the past few years, a number of parties in the United States and abroad have questioned whether larger backbone providers are able to gain or exploit market power through the terms of interconnection that they offer to smaller existing and new backbone providers. In addition, backbones may attempt in the future to differentiate themselves from their competitors by not interconnecting at all to exchange traffic flowing from innovative new services. The paper shows how competition, governed by antitrust laws and competition enforcement that can prevent the emergence of a dominant firm, can act to restrain the actions of larger backbones in place of any industry-specific regulations, such as interconnection obligations.

Section two of this paper examines the history of Internet interconnection and describes current interconnection policies between Internet backbones. The paper next examines several current and potential pressures on the domestic system of interconnection in section three, while section four examines international interconnection issues. The conclusion is in section five.

II. Background

A. Introduction

This paper examines the interconnection arrangements that enable each Internet user to communicate with every other Internet user.[2] For simplicity, the paper focuses on the interactions between four groups of Internet participants: end users, content providers, Internet service providers (ISPs), and Internet backbone providers (backbones). End users communicate

---

[1] For purposes of this paper, industry-specific regulations are defined to be rules, applied by an expert agency, that govern the behavior of companies in a particular industry. These regulations supplement the antitrust laws and ordinary common law rules that apply to all industries in the United States. In general, industry-specific regulations correct for market failures that antitrust laws and ordinary common laws cannot resolve or prevent. In this paper, an "unregulated" industry is one that is not subject to any industry-specific regulations.

[2] For further discussion of the structure of the Internet, *see* Kevin Werbach, "Digital Tornado: the Internet and Telecommunications Policy" (OPP Working Paper Series No. 29, 1997)(Digital Tornado) at 10-12. *See also* Jean-Jacques Laffont and Jean Tirole, *Competition in Telecommunications* (MIT Press, 2000) at 268-272; J. Scott Marcus, *Designing Wide Area Networks and Internetworks: A Practical Guide*, (Addison Wesley Longman, 1999)(*Designing Wide Area Networks*) at 274-289.

with each other using the Internet, and also access information or purchase products or services from content providers, such as the Wall Street Journal Interactive Edition, or e-commerce vendors, such as Amazon.com. End users access the Internet via Internet service providers such as America Online (AOL) or MindSpring Enterprises. Small business and residential end users generally use modems to connect to their ISP over standard telephone lines, while larger businesses and content providers generally have dedicated access to their ISP over leased lines.[3] Content providers use a dedicated connection to the Internet that offers end users twenty-four hour access to their content. ISPs are generally connected to other ISPs through Internet backbone providers such as UUNET and PSINet. Backbones own or lease national or international high-speed fiber optic networks that are connected by routers, which the backbones use to deliver traffic to and from their customers. Many backbones also are vertically integrated, functioning as ISPs by selling Internet access directly to end users, as well as having ISPs as customers.

Each backbone provider essentially forms its own network that enables all connected end users and content providers to communicate with one another. End users, however, are generally not interested in communicating just with end users and content providers connected to the same backbone provider; rather, they want to be able to communicate with a wide variety of end users and content providers, regardless of backbone provider. In order to provide end users with such universal connectivity, backbones must interconnect with one another to exchange traffic destined for each other's end users. It is this interconnection that makes the Internet the "network of networks" that it is today. As a result of widespread interconnection, end users currently have an implicit expectation of universal connectivity whenever they log on to the Internet, regardless of which ISP they choose. ISPs are therefore in the business of selling access to the entire Internet to their end-user customers; ISPs purchase this universal access from Internet backbones. The driving force behind the need for these firms to deliver access to the whole Internet to customers is what is known in the economics literature as *network externalities*.

B. Network Externalities

Network externalities arise when the value, or utility, that a consumer derives from a product or service increases as a function of the number of other consumers of the same or compatible products or services.[4] They are called network externalities because they generally arise for networks whose purpose it is to enable each user to communicate with other users; as a result, by definition the more users there are, the more valuable the network.[5] These benefits are

---

[3]   A leased line is an access line rented for the exclusive use of the customer; with dedicated access to an ISP, the customer can be logged on to the Internet twenty-four hours a day. New broadband access technologies, such as xDSL and cable modems, are increasingly replacing traditional dial-up modems, enabling residential and small business customers to receive the same high-speed "always-on" access to the Internet enjoyed by dedicated access customers.

[4]   *See* Michael L. Katz and Carl Shapiro, "Systems Competition and Network Effects," *Journal of Economic Perspectives*, Vol. 8, No. 2, Spring 1994, at 93-115; Nicholas Economides, "The Economics of Networks," *International Journal of Industrial Organization*, Vol. 14, No. 2, March 1996.

[5]   Metcalfe's law, which states that the value of a network grows in proportion to the square of the number of users of the network, is a specific expression of network externalities. *See* Harry Newton, *Newton's Telecom Dictionary* (Flatiron Publishing, (14th ed.), 1998)(*Newton's*) at 447-448.

externalities because a user, when deciding whether to join a network (or which network to join), only takes into account the private benefits that the network will bring her, and will not consider the fact that her joining this network increases the benefit of the network for other users. This latter effect is an externality.

Network externalities can be direct or indirect. Network externalities are direct for networks that consumers use to communicate with one another; the more consumers that use the network, the more valuable the network is for each consumer.[6] The phone system is a classic example of a system providing direct network externalities. The only benefit of such a system comes from access to the network of users. Network externalities are indirect for systems that require both hardware and software in order to provide benefits.[7] As more consumers buy hardware, this will lead to the production of more software compatible with this hardware, making the hardware more valuable to users. A classic example of this is the compact disc system; as more consumers purchased compact disc players, music companies increased the variety of compact discs available, making the players more valuable to their owners.[8] These network externalities are indirect because consumers do not purchase the systems to communicate directly with others, yet they benefit indirectly from the adoption decision of other consumers.

One unique characteristic of the Internet is that it offers both direct and indirect network externalities. Users of applications such as email and Internet telephony derive direct network externalities from the system: the more Internet users there are, the more valuable the Internet is for such communications. Users of applications such as the World Wide Web derive indirect network externalities from the system: the more Internet users there are, the more Web content will be developed, which makes the Internet even more valuable for its users. The ability to provide direct and indirect network externalities to customers provides an almost overpowering incentive for Internet backbones to cooperate with one another by interconnecting their networks.

C. Peering and Transit

During the early development of the Internet, there was only one backbone, and therefore interconnection between backbones was not an issue.[9] In 1986, the National Science Foundation (NSF) funded the NSFNET, a 56-kilobit per second (Kbps) network created to enable long-distance access to five supercomputer centers across the country. In 1987, a partnership of Merit Network, Inc., IBM, and MCI began to manage the NSFNET, which became a T-1 network

---

[6]   *See* Michael L. Katz and Carl Shapiro, "Network Externalities, Competition, and Compatibility," *American Economic Review*, Vol. 75, June 1985 ("Network Externalities") at 424-440.

[7]   *See* Jeffrey Church and Neil Gandal, "Network Effects, Software Provision, and Standardization," *Journal of Industrial Economics*, Vol. 40, March 1992, at 85-104.

[8]   For an empirical description of the interplay between compact disc hardware sales and the availability of compact discs, *see* Neil Gandal, Michael Kende, and Rafael Rob, "The Dynamics of Technological Adoption in Hardware/Software Systems: The Case of Compact Disc Players," *Rand Journal of Economics*, Vol. 31, No. 1, Spring 2000, at 43-61.

[9]   *See* Werbach, "Digital Tornado" at 13-16 for a brief history of the Internet. *See also* Robert H'obbes' Zakon, Hobbes' Internet Timeline v4.1," http://www.isoc.org/guest/zakon/Internet/History/HIT html.

connecting thirteen sites in 1988.[10] The issue of interconnection arose only when a number of commercial backbones came into being, and eventually supplanted the NSFNET.[11]

At the time that commercial networks began appearing, general commercial activity on the NSFNET was prohibited by an Acceptable Use Policy, thereby preventing these commercial networks from exchanging traffic with one another using the NSFNET as the backbone. This roadblock was circumvented in 1991, when a number of commercial backbone operators including PSINet, UUNET, and CerfNET established the Commercial Internet Exchange (CIX). CIX consisted of a router, housed in Santa Clara, California, that was set up for the purpose of interconnecting these commercial backbones and enabling them to exchange their end users' traffic. In 1993, the NSF decided to leave the management of the backbone entirely to competing, commercial backbones. In order to facilitate the growth of overlapping competing backbones, the NSF designed a system of geographically dispersed Network Access Points (NAPs) similar to CIX, each consisting of a shared switch or local area network (LAN) used to exchange traffic. The four original NAPs were in San Francisco (operated by PacBell), Chicago (BellCore and Ameritech), New York (SprintLink) and Washington, D.C. (MFS). Backbones could choose to interconnect with one another at any or all of these NAPs. In 1995, this network of commercial backbones and NAPs permanently replaced the NSFNET.

The interconnection of commercial backbones is not subject to any industry-specific regulations. The NSF did not establish any interconnection rules at the NAPs, and interconnection between Internet backbone providers is not currently regulated by the Federal Communications Commission or any other government agency.[12] Instead, interconnection arrangements evolved from the informal interactions that characterized the Internet at the time the NSF was running the backbone. The commercial backbones developed a system of interconnection known as peering. Peering has a number of distinctive characteristics. First, peering partners only exchange traffic that originates with the customer of one backbone and terminates with the customer of the other peered backbone. In Figure 1, customers of backbones *A* and *C* can trade traffic as a result of a peering relationship between the backbones, as can the customers of backbones *B* and *C*, which also have a peering arrangement. As part of a peering arrangement, a backbone would not, however, act as an intermediary and accept the traffic of one peering partner and transit this traffic to another peering partner.[13] Thus, referring back to Figure 1, backbone *C* will not accept traffic from backbone *A* destined for backbone *B*. The second distinctive characteristic of peering is that peering partners exchange traffic on a settlements-free basis.[14] The only costs that backbones incur to peer is that each partner pays for its own equipment and the transmission capacity needed for the two peers to meet at each peering point.

Additional characteristics of peering relate to the routing of information from one backbone to another. Peering partners generally meet in a number of geographically dispersed locations. In order to decide where to pass traffic from one backbone to another in a consistent

---

[10]   A T-1 network carries 1.544 megabits of data per second (Mbps).

[11]   *See* Janet Abbate, *Inventing the Internet*, (MIT Press, 1999) at 191-200.

[12]   For a discussion of the FCC's role in the Internet, *see* Jason Oxman, "The FCC and the Unregulation of the Internet," (OPP Working Paper Series No. 31, 1999)(Unregulation of the Internet).

[13]   *See, e.g.,* Intermedia Communications "Peering White Paper," 1998, http://www.intermedia.com (Intermedia White Paper) at n.1, for a definition of peering.

[14]   This is similar to bill-and-keep or sender-keeps-all arrangements. *See infra* n. 26.

and fair manner, they have adopted what is known as "hot-potato routing," whereby a backbone will pass traffic to another backbone at the earliest point of exchange.[15] As an example, in Figure 5 backbones *A* and *B* are interconnected on the West and East coasts. When a customer of ISP *X* on the East coast requests a web page from a site connected to ISP *Y* on the West coast, backbone *A* passes this request to backbone *B* on the East coast, and backbone *B* carries this request to the West coast. Likewise, the responding web page is routed from backbone *B* to backbone *A* on the West coast, and backbone *A* is responsible for carrying the response to the customer of ISP *X* on the East coast. A final characteristic of peering is that recipients of traffic only promise to undertake "best efforts" when terminating traffic, rather than guarantee any level of performance in delivering packets received from peering partners.

The original system of peering has evolved over time. Initially, most exchange of traffic under peering arrangements took place at the NAPs, as it was efficient for each backbone to interconnect with as many backbones as possible at the same location, as shown in the example in Figure 2. Each backbone must only provide a connection to one point, the NAP, rather than providing individual connections to every other backbone. The rapid growth in Internet traffic soon caused the NAPs to become congested, however, which led to delayed and dropped packets. For instance, Intermedia Business Solutions asserts that at one point packet loss at the Washington, D.C. NAP reached up to 20 percent.[16] As a result, a number of new NAPs have appeared to reduce the amount of traffic flowing through the original NAPs. For example, MFS, now owned by WorldCom, operates a number of NAPs known as Metropolitan Area Exchanges (MAEs), including one of the original NAPs, the Washington, D.C. NAP known as MAE-East, as well as MAE-West in San Jose, and other MAEs in Los Angeles, Dallas, and Chicago.

Another result of the increased congestion at the NAPs has been that many backbones began to interconnect directly with one another.[17] This system has come to be known as *private peering*, as opposed to the public peering that takes place at the NAPs. In Figure 3, backbones *A* and *B* have established a private peering connection through which they bypass the NAP when exchanging traffic for each other – they both only use the NAP when exchanging traffic with backbone *C*.[18] This system developed partly in response to congestion at the NAPs, yet it may often be more cost-effective for the backbones.[19] For instance, if backbones were to interconnect only at NAPs, traffic that originated and terminated in the same city but on different backbones would have to travel to a NAP in a different city or even a different country for exchange.[20] With private peering, in contrast, it can be exchanged within the same city. This alleviates the strain on the NAPs. At one point it was estimated that 80 percent of Internet traffic was

---

[15]   *See* J. Scott Marcus, *Designing Wide Area Networks*, at 283-285.
[16]   Intermedia White Paper at 2.
[17]   *See* J. Scott Marcus, *Designing Wide Area Networks*, at 280-282.
[18]   Private peering may take place in the same physical location as the NAP. If two carriers wishing to peer privately already have transport going to a NAP, they may simply bypass the NAP's switches and interconnect directly at the same location.
[19]   For instance, Intermedia states that its "dual peering policy," combining open public peering with private peering, "will create a win-win solution for everyone and a better management approach to the Internet." Intermedia White Paper at 3.
[20]   Prior to the establishment of a NAP in Rome, for example, backbones often exchanged domestic Italian Internet traffic in the United States. Sam Paltridge, Working Party on Telecommunication and Information Services Policies, "Internet Traffic Exchange: Developments and Policy," OECD, 1998 (OECD Report) at 22-23.

exchanged via private peering.[21] There are recent indications, however, that as NAPs begin to switch to Asynchronous Transfer Mode (ATM)[22] and other advanced switch technologies, the NAPs will be able to provide higher quality services and may regain their former attraction as efficient meeting points for peering partners.[23] Unless specified, discussions of peering below refer to both public and private peering.

Because each bilateral peering arrangement only allows backbones to exchange traffic destined for each other's customers, backbones need a significant number of peering arrangements in order to gain access to the full Internet. UUNET, for instance, claims to "peer with 75 other ISPs globally."[24] As discussed below, there are few backbones that rely solely on private or public peering to meet their interconnection needs. The alternative to peering is a transit arrangement between backbones, in which one backbone pays another backbone to deliver traffic between its customers and the customers of other backbones.

Transit and peering are differentiated in two main ways. First, in a transit arrangement, one backbone pays another backbone for interconnection, and therefore becomes a wholesale customer of the other backbone. Second, unlike in a peering relationship, with transit, the backbone selling the transit services will route traffic from the transit customer to its peering partners. In Figure 4, backbone *A* is a transit customer of backbone *C*; thus, the customers of backbone *A* have access both to the customers of backbone *C* as well as to the customers of all peering partners of backbone *C*, such as backbone *B*. If backbone *A* and backbone *C* were peering partners, as in Figure 1, backbone *C* would not accept traffic from backbone *A* that was destined for backbone *B*.

Many backbones have adopted a hybrid approach to interconnection, peering with a number of backbones and paying for transit from one or more backbones in order to have access to the backbone of the transit supplier as well as the peering partners of the transit supplier. Those few large backbones that interconnect solely by peering, and do not need to purchase transit from any other backbones, will be referred to here as *top-tier backbones*. Because of the non-disclosure agreements that cover interconnection between backbones, it is difficult to state with accuracy the number of top-tier backbones; according to one industry participant, there are five: Cable & Wireless, WorldCom, Sprint, AT&T, and Genuity (formerly GTE Internetworking).[25]

---

[21]   Michael Gaddis, chief technical officer of SAVVIS Communications, gave this estimate. Randy Barrett, "ISP Survival Guide," inter@ctive week online, December 7, 1998.

[22]   ATM is a "high bandwidth, low-delay, connection oriented, packet-like switching and multiplexing technique." *Newton's* at 67-69.

[23]   *See* J. Scott Marcus, *Designing Wide Area Networks*, at 278. Marcus states that "[I]n 1998, MCI WorldCom upgraded its MAE facilities … to offer modern ATM switches as a high-capacity alternative to the FDDI/gigaswitch architecture." *See also* Letter from Attorneys for MCI WorldCom and Sprint to Magalie Roman Salas, Secretary, FCC, Attach. at 20-21 (filed January 14, 2000 in CC Docket No. 99-333, *Application for Consent to the Transfer of Control of Licenses from Sprint Corporation to MCI WorldCom, Inc.*)(MCI WorldCom Sprint Jan. 14, 2000, *Ex Parte*)("In short, the deployment of ATM switches has expanded the capability of NAPs to handle the demand for public peering by increasing the number of ports as well as the capacity available at NAPs.")

[24]   MCI WorldCom Sprint Jan. 14, 2000, *Ex Parte*, Attach at 20, n. 48.

[25]   J. Scott Marcus, *Designing Wide Area Networks*, at 280. Marcus is the Chief Technology Officer of Genuity. Genuity was formerly GTE Internetworking. In order to comply with Section 271 of the Telecommunications Act of 1996, and thereby obtain Commission approval to merge with Bell Atlantic, GTE agreed to sell most of its equity in Genuity to the public through an initial public offering. "Bell Atlantic and GTE

It is useful to compare Internet interconnection arrangements with more familiar, traditional telephony interconnection arrangements. The practice of peering is similar to the practice of bill-and-keep or sender-keeps-all arrangements in telephony.[26] Transit arrangements between Internet backbones are somewhat similar to resale arrangements between, for instance, long distance carriers; the Internet backbone providing transit service acts as the wholesaler, and the backbone buying transit acts as the reseller of Internet backbone services. There are notable differences in the way Internet and telephony arrangements are regulated, however. The interconnection between Internet backbones is not governed by industry-specific regulations, while the interconnection of traditional telephone carriers is currently regulated both domestically and internationally. Furthermore, unlike telephony, there is no difference between domestic and international Internet interconnection arrangements; backbones treat each other the same regardless of the country of origin or location of customer base.[27]

There is no accepted convention that governs when two backbones will or should decide to peer with one another, nor is it an easy matter to devise one. The term "peer" suggests equality, and one convention could be that backbones of equal size would peer. However, there are many measures of backbone size, such as geographic spread, capacity, traffic volume, or number of customers. It is unlikely that two backbones will be similar along many or all dimensions. One may have fewer, but larger, customers than the other, another may reach into Europe or Asia, and so forth. The question then becomes, how the backbones weigh one variable against another. Given the complexity of such judgments, it may be best to use a definition of equality proposed by one industry participant -- that companies will peer when they perceive equal benefit from peering based on their own subjective terms, rather than any objective terms.[28] In sum, peering agreements are the result of commercial negotiations; each backbone bases its decisions on whether, how, and where to peer by weighing the benefits and costs of entering into a particular interconnection agreement with another backbone.

The paper now examines why there are no industry-specific regulations governing interconnection between Internet backbone providers today, before turning to a study of the interactions between backbone providers in this unregulated market.

Chairmen Praise FCC Merger Approval," GTE Press Release, June 16, 2000. In addition, according to Marcus, "somewhere between six and perhaps thirty other ISPs could also be viewed as backbone ISPs." *Id.* Marcus states that "the ability to reach all Internet destinations without the need for a transit relationship … is a strong indicator that an ISP should be viewed as a backbone ISP." *Id.* at 279. This is similar to the definition used in this paper of a top-tier backbone.

[26] In a bill-and-keep or sender-keep-all arrangement, each carrier bills its own customers for the origination of traffic and does not pay the other carrier for terminating this traffic. In a settlement arrangement, on the other hand, the carrier on which the traffic originates pays the other carrier to terminate the traffic. If traffic flows between the two networks are balanced, the net settlement that each pays is zero, and therefore a bill-and-keep arrangement may be preferred because the networks do not have to incur costs to measure and track traffic or to develop billing systems. As an example, the Telecommunications Act of 1996 allows for incumbent local exchange carriers to exchange traffic with competitors using a bill-and-keep arrangement. 47 U.S.C. § 252 (d)(2)(B)(i). *See also infra* at n. 105.

[27] *See infra* at Section IV, International Interconnection Issues.

[28] Geoff Huston, "Interconnection, Peering and Settlements," January 1999, http://www.telstra net/gih/peerdocs/peer.html at 3-4. *See also* J. Scott Marcus, *Designing Wide Area Networks* at 279. ("Over time, it came to be recognized that peers need not be similar in size; rather, what was important was that there be comparable value in the traffic exchanged.").

D. The Backbone as an Unregulated Service

The Federal Communications Commission maintains a policy to "focus on sustaining competitive communications markets and protecting the public interest where markets fail to do so."[29] As an example of this policy, for many years the FCC has recognized a categorical distinction between regulated telecommunications services and unregulated computer-based services.[30] To understand why Internet backbone services are, and should continue to be, treated as unregulated services, it is important to highlight two basic policies. First, it is important to understand the basis for the regulation of network industries. For the telecommunications network, like the railroad and the telegraph before it, to grow into a healthy and vibrant universally available network, striking a "common carrier" bargain with telephone companies was a beneficial government intervention. In addition, given the economies of scale inherent in the construction of the telecommunications network, natural monopoly regulation was necessary to ensure reasonable price and quality levels. Second, it is important to understand why certain services are not regulated as common carrier services. Soon after their introduction, the FCC determined that the computer-based services market would remain competitive, and therefore should not be regulated, so long as an essential input to such services – telecommunications capability – was available to providers of such services on a nondiscriminatory basis. Thus it was not necessary to impose common carrier regulations on the users of those telecommunications services as well as the providers. The following is a brief overview of relevant domestic telecommunications regulations.[31]

1. Common Carrier Regulation

The traditional rationale for regulating network industries, such as telecommunications, was the almost overwhelming economies of scale in the provision of such services.[32] Economic theory and practice suggests that a natural monopolist is likely to arise in such industries; this is considered efficient to the extent that duplicative facilities are not installed.[33] However, without competitors, a natural monopoly can harm consumers in a variety of ways, which fall generally into three categories: 1) the monopolist can directly raise retail prices and/or reduce retail service quality; 2) the monopolist can leverage market power into related markets that would otherwise

---

[29]   "A New FCC for the 21st Century," *Draft Strategic Plan* (August 1999), http://www.fcc.gov/21st_century, at 3.

[30]   *See e.g.* Jason Oxman, "Unregulation of the Internet."

[31]   *See also* Gerald R. Brock, *Telecommunications Policy for the Information Age: from Monopoly to Competition* (Harvard University Press, 1994)(*Telecommunications Policy*); Ingo Vogelsang and Bridger M. Mitchell, *Telecommunications Competition: The Last Ten Miles* (The MIT Press and The AEI Press, 1997)(*Telecommunications Competition*).

[32]   Economies of scale arise when the cost per unit of providing service decreases as output increases. In wireline telephony there are enormous economies of scale resulting from the network of copper loops that serve homes and businesses. The cost of having one company serve a particular area was historically much lower than having two or more companies with partial or full overbuilds of each other's networks. Lately, new technologies have altered the traditional cost structures in a number of network industries such as telephony, which enabled the pro-competitive, deregulatory provisions of the Telecommunications Act of 1996.

[33]   *See* Robert S. Pindyck and Daniel L. Rubinfeld, *Microeconomics*, (Prentice Hall, 4th ed. 1998) at 352-358.

be competitive;[34] and 3) the monopolist can deny access to its network and thus bar entry into its core markets.

Governments worldwide traditionally chose to operate or regulate natural monopolies in order to benefit from the efficiencies inherent in having a single provider, while not incurring the corresponding harms that the natural monopolies could inflict on consumers. In the United States, certain telecommunications providers have been subject to natural monopoly regulation; this meant a government grant of monopoly (the monopoly granted to local telephone companies, for example, was lifted by Congress in 1996), along with rate and service quality regulation. In addition, all telecommunications providers, even those not subject to natural monopoly regulation, are regulated as common carriers, as described below. It should be noted that the goals of regulation are similar to those of antitrust policy -- both seek to protect consumers from firms with market power. Indeed, in the United States, federal antitrust actions preceded the imposition of telecommunications regulation, and have since served to supplement those regulations. Broadly speaking, in the United States regulatory approaches have been used to control firms' actions while taking the market structure as given; antitrust policy has been used to control firms' actions by acting on the market structure itself, such as by reviewing mergers that would increase market concentration, inducing a divestiture aimed at reducing concentration, or preventing firms from taking actions that cripple market mechanisms.[35] For the public, the sum of these approaches brought the beneficial construction of a nationwide telecommunications network while ensuring affordable access to that network for all users.

Government involvement in the nascent telephone market began at the turn of the 20th century. Even before the passage of the Communications Act in 1934, the Supreme Court ruled that telegraph companies had a duty – arising out of the common law – to serve all customers in a nondiscriminatory manner as a common carrier.[36] In addition, thirty-four states determined that mandating interconnection obligations was the best way to resolve disputes that had arisen between 1894 and 1906 between the Bell System, the largest telephone company at the time, and smaller independent telephone companies. It was not until 1910 that the Mann-Elkins Act extended the jurisdiction of the Interstate Commerce Commission to include telephone companies.[37] In 1913, in response to a threatened antitrust case, AT&T entered into an agreement, known as the Kingsbury Commitment, to interconnect with independent local

---

[34] For instance, local wireline services are necessary inputs in the provision of wireless and long distance services; a carrier with market power over local services could leverage this market power into these related markets.

[35] In the United States, two agencies have overlapping jurisdiction to enforce federal antitrust policy -- the Federal Trade Commission (FTC) and the Department of Justice (DOJ). In telecommunications, the Federal Communications Commission, the federal agency charged with regulating interstate communications by wire and radio, has authority pursuant to the Communications Act to determine whether transactions involving the transfer of certain licenses or authorizations serve the public interest. *See Applications of Ameritech Corp., Transferor, and SBC Communications Inc., Transferee, For Consent to Transfer Control of Corporations Holding Commission Licenses and Lines Pursuant to Sections 214 and 310(d) of the Communications Act and Parts 5, 22, 24, 25, 63, 90, 95 and 101 of the Commission's Rules*, CC Docket No. 98-141, Memorandum Opinion and Order, (rel. Oct. 8, 1999) at paras. 46-54. The Commission also shares concurrent antitrust jurisdiction with DOJ under the Clayton Act to review mergers between common carriers. *Id.* at para. 53.

[36] *See Western Union Tel. Co. v. Call Publishing Co.*, 181 U.S. 92, 99-104 (1901).

[37] Mann-Elkins Act, Pub. L. No. 61-218, 36 Stat. 539 (1910).

telephone companies for long distance calls.[38] In 1934, Congress established the Federal Communications Commission to regulate telecommunications common carriers.[39]

Today, pursuant to the Communications Act, as amended, communications common carriers must offer service on demand to the public at large without unreasonable discrimination.[40] Common carriers with market power are subject to additional regulations that restrict rates and govern service quality levels. In order to prevent common carriers with market power from leveraging this market power into related competitive markets, including long distance and the manufacture of consumer premise equipment (CPE), there have a been a wide range of regulations, including outright divestiture and prohibition on entering these related markets. Where the entering of such markets is permitted, it is often subject to regulations that ensure non discrimination between affiliates of the carrier with market power and unaffiliated providers. As competition is introduced into formerly monopolized telecommunications markets such as local telephony, regulation is nevertheless required in order to encourage the incumbent monopolist to open its network fully to potential entrants.

Over the years, technological advances have altered the cost structure upon which natural monopoly regulation rested. The regulatory response in the United States has been to relax regulation in markets where competition has eliminated the need for regulation, while protecting these markets from firms with market power in related segments of the industry.[41] As an example, after upstarts such as MCI demonstrated that competition was possible in the provision of long distance services, an antitrust case brought by the Department of Justice culminated in the breakup of the Bell System into AT&T, providing long distance services in a competitive market, and the seven Regional Bell Operating Companies (RBOCs) providing local services in exclusive regions.[42] The RBOCs were prohibited from entering long distance markets in order to prevent the discrimination towards unaffiliated long distance carriers that lead to the breakup of the Bell System in the first place. Recently, as competition became possible in local markets, Congress passed the Telecommunications Act of 1996 (1996 Act), requiring incumbent Local Exchange Carriers (LECs), such as the RBOCs and GTE, to open their local markets to competition by a variety of means.[43] These requirements are crucial to the

---

[38]   See Vogelsang and Mitchell, *Telecommunications Competition*, at 64.

[39]   The Communications Act of 1934, the Federal Communication Commission's enabling statute, created the Commission "for the purpose of regulating interstate and foreign commerce in communication by wire and radio ..." and established "the public interest, convenience, and necessity" as the principles that guide Commission decisionmaking. The Communications Act defines a common carrier as "any person engaged as a common carrier for hire." 47 U.S.C. § 153(h).

[40]   In exchange, there is protection from certain types of liability. *See, e.g., Richman Bros. Records v. FCC*, 124 F.3d 1302 (D.C. Cir. 1997).

[41]   See, e.g., *Policy and Rules Concerning Rates for Competitive Common Carrier Services and Facilities Authorizations Therefor,* First Report and Order, 85 FCC 2d 1 (1980) ("Application of current regulatory procedures to non-dominant carriers imposes unnecessary and counterproductive regulatory constraints upon a marketplace that can satisfy consumer demand without government intervention."). *See also Motion of AT&T Corp. to be Reclassified as a Non-dominant Carrier*, Order, 11 FCC Rcd 3271 (1995) (determining that AT&T should be declared non dominant).

[42]   See *United States v. American Tel. & Tel. Co.*, 552 F. Supp. 131 (D.D.C. 1982). *See also* Vogelsang and Mitchell, *Telecommunications Competition*, at 67-69; Brock, *Telecommunications Policy for the Information Age*, at Chpt. 9.

[43]   The 1996 Act provides for three types of competition: facilities-based competition, competition using network elements unbundled (leased) from the incumbent at cost-based rates, and competition reselling the

development of a competitive telecommunications network, and the Federal Communications Commission rules implementing these requirements will be relaxed as competition renders them unnecessary.[44]

In summary, telecommunications providers are subject to common carrier regulations that ensure nondiscriminatory access to end users; together with antitrust enforcement, these regulations serve to protect against anti-competitive behavior by telecommunications providers with market power. In markets where competition can act in place of regulation as the means to protect consumers from the exercise of market power, the Commission has long chosen to abstain from imposing regulation. For this reason, providers of services that combine telecommunications with computer services are not regulated as common carriers.

2. Basic versus Enhanced Services

For more than thirty years, the Commission has sought to avoid imposing unnecessary common carrier regulation on providers of computer services that rely on the nation's telecommunications infrastructure for transmission of those services, but do not themselves provide telecommunications services to the public. The absence of market power in the computer services industry led the Commission to conclude that imposing common carrier regulation was unnecessary and might discourage innovation and distort the nascent data marketplace. The Commission instead focused on ensuring that the providers of the underlying telecommunications services made these services available on a non discriminatory basis and did not themselves leverage their market power into the provision of these complementary computer services. As a result, the competitive enhanced services market was able to flourish without onerous regulations impeding its growth.

In 1966, the Commission opened the *Computer Inquiry* proceeding that explored the regulatory and policy issues raised by the nascent interdependence of computer and communication technologies. In announcing the inquiry, the Commission foreshadowed the incredible attributes of computer networks that would make the Internet such a valuable tool.

> The modern day electronic computer is capable of being programmed to furnish a wide variety of services, including the processing of all kinds of data and the gathering, storage forwarding, and retrieval of information – technical, statistical, medical, cultural, among numerous other classes. With its huge capacity and versatility, the computer is capable of providing its services to a multiplicity of users at locations remote from the computer. Effective use of the computer is, therefore, becoming increasingly dependent upon communication common carrier facilities and services by which the computers and the user are given instantaneous access to each other.[45]

---

incumbent's service. To ensure that the customers of the competitors remain plugged into the network, section 251 of the 1996 Act requires that incumbent LECs offer nondiscriminatory interconnection terms and conditions to competitors. *See* 47 U.S.C. § 251. Absent such a requirement, incumbents would be able to deny competitors access to their monopoly networks.

[44] Upon a showing that local markets are open to competition, the RBOCs are granted authority to enter the market for long distance services, pursuant to section 271 of the 1996 Act. 47 U.S.C. § 271.

[45] *First Computer Inquiry*, 7 FCC 2d 11, para. 1.

In the early 1970s, the Commission determined that there were "no natural or economic barriers to free entry into the market for [computer] services."[46] The Commission therefore decided that the policies and objectives of the Communications Act would best be served by allowing computer services to operate in an environment free from industry-specific regulation. In addition, the Commission devised rules that require common carriers to grant nondiscriminatory access to their networks to enhanced service providers. Mandating such nondiscrimination, the Commission concluded, was necessary because the computer-based service industry "cannot survive, much less develop further, except through reliance upon and use of communications facilities and services."[47]

In order to facilitate the implementation of its computer services policy, the Commission created the categories of "basic" and "enhanced" services.[48] The basic services category denotes common carrier services subject to Title II of the Communications Act.[49] The enhanced services category denotes those services

> offered over common carrier transmission facilities used in interstate communications, which employ computer processing applications that act on the format, content, code, protocol, or similar aspects of the subscriber's transmitted information, provide the subscriber additional, different, or restructured information; or involve subscriber interaction with stored information.[50]

Thus, a basic service is a communications pathway, like a telephone line, while an enhanced service is a computer-enhanced offering that operates via that communications pathway. Present day examples of unregulated enhanced services include voicemail services, gateway services, electronic publishing, and Internet services. In these markets, competition between firms, rather than any industry-specific regulations, ensures that consumers enjoy low prices and innovative services.

E. Growth of the Internet Industry

In the past five years, the Internet has experienced unprecedented growth rates. The market for Internet backbone services has grown since privatization in 1995 into a market with a multitude of competing providers.[51] Figure 7 shows that, according to *Boardwatch* magazine,

---

[46]   *First Computer Inquiry*, Tentative Decision, 28 FCC 2d at para. 18.

[47]   *First Computer Inquiry*, Final Decision and Order, 28 FCC 2d at 7.

[48]   The 1996 Act introduced new provisions referring to "telecommunications service" and "information service." For definitions of these services, *see* 47. U.S.C. § 153(46) and 153(20), respectively. The Commission has concluded that these definitions correspond to the categories of basic and enhanced services, respectively. For a general discussion, *see In the Matter of Federal-State Joint Board on Universal Service*, CC Docket No. 96-45, Report to Congress, 13 FCC Rcd 11501 (1998).

[49]   Basic services are defined as a common carrier offering of a pure "transmission capacity for the movement of information." *Amendment of Section 64.702 of the Commission's Rules and Regulations (Second Computer Inquiry)*, 77 FCC 2d 384, 419 (1980) (*Computer II Final Decision*).

[50]   47 C.F.R. § 64.702(a).

[51]   The analysis contained in this paper is based solely on publicly available information. As in most markets, information about Internet backbone prices and costs is proprietary. In addition, information about the nature of relationships between Internet backbone providers is protected by non-disclosure agreements. The effects of these non-disclosure agreements on this analysis are described below.

there are forty-two national backbones, a number that has been rising steadily since the Internet was privatized.[52] *Boardwatch* defines a national backbone to be one "maintaining a hub city in at least five different states, spanning both coasts, and peering at the major NAPs."[53] The list of national backbones includes the top-tier backbones that only peer with other backbones, as well as other smaller national backbones that peer with some backbones and purchase transit from others. Due to the non-disclosure agreements covering contracts between backbones, it is impossible to know the exact breakdown between the number of top-tier backbones and other national backbones, although there are suggestions that there are five top-tier backbones.[54]

The list of national backbones includes a number of backbones that pre-date the privatization of the Internet, as well as a number of newer players that have entered partly on the strength of their new fiber facilities.[55] Many of the older backbones have been swept into the merger wave that is now transforming the general communications industry, and, combined with their merger partners, remain among the largest backbones. WorldCom now owns UUNET and ANS Communications, two of the earliest backbones, along with GridNet, Unicom-Pipex, InNet, NL Net, and Metrix Interlink.[56] UUNET, in turn, owns MFS Communications, which runs the NAPs known as MAEs, including one of the original NAPs, MAE East. According to the Department of Justice, UUNET is now "by far the largest provider of Internet backbone services in the world, whether measured by traffic or revenues."[57] In 1997, GTE Internetworking, since renamed Genuity, purchased BBN, the developer of a precursor to the modern day Internet, and was then spun off as a separate public corporation.[58] AT&T's role in the backbone market has grown with its purchases of CERFnet, another early backbone, along with IBM's Global Network business. Cable & Wireless entered the ranks of the largest backbones when it purchased MCI's Internet backbone, which was divested during the MCI WorldCom merger proceeding.[59] Finally, PSINet, an early backbone that has remained independent, also remains among the list of the larger backbones.

The increase in the number of backbones has been facilitated by the recent dramatic increases in the availability of fiber optic capacity. Figure 11 shows that, not only have the fiber networks owned by the incumbent carriers -- AT&T, Sprint, and MCI WorldCom -- all grown in recent years, a more significant increase in capacity comes from four entrants -- Qwest, Broadwing (formerly IXC), Williams, and Level 3 -- that have built or are building nationwide fiber optic networks.[60] Not only are these four companies themselves national Internet

---

[52]   In 1999, *Boardwatch* actually listed forty-three national backbones, however, for purposes of this paper we count as one backbone the two backbones listed as owned by MCI WorldCom -- Advanced Networks and UUNET. In addition, *Boardwatch* does not include in its list five other national backbones, Williams Communications, Bell Canada/Bell Nexxia, Network Two, ITC DeltaCom, and RoadRunner, because these backbones would not release their prices. For consistency with *Boardwatch*'s previous lists, these backbones are not accounted for here. *Boardwatch Magazine's Directory of Internet Service Providers*, 11th ed., 1999, at 5.

[53]   *Boardwatch Magazine Directory of Internet Service Providers*, Vol. 2, Fall 1997, at 27.

[54]   *See supra* at n. 25.

[55]   *See Boardwatch Magazine's Directory of Internet Service Providers*, 11th ed., 1999, for a complete list and description of national backbone providers.

[56]   *See United States of America v. WorldCom, Inc. and Sprint Corporation*, Complaint (DOJ WorldCom Sprint Complaint), June 27, 2000, p. 6.

[57]   *Id.* at pp. 4-5.

[58]   *See supra* at n. 25.

[59]   *See infra* at n. 67.

[60]   IXC Communications merged with Cincinnati Bell to become Broadwing Inc.

backbones, but a number of other backbones have in turn bought or leased capacity from them. For instance, PSINet purchased sixteen fibers covering 14,000 miles from the former IXC Communications.[61] Backbones also lease fiber capacity from facilities-based carriers. The development of dense wavelength division multiplexing (DWDM) technologies, which divide each strand of fiber into multiple channels, is further increasing the availability of fiber capacity by multiplying the capacity of existing and new networks. Entry into the backbone market is facilitated by this increasing availability of fiber capacity from a growing number of providers.

The growth in private Internet backbones has coincided with the introduction of the World Wide Web, which has popularized the Internet for millions of consumers. The result is a virtuous cycle that is typical of industries characterized by network externalities. In this case, users, drawn to the Internet by applications such as the World Wide Web, encourage the creation of more Web content, which in turn encourages additional users to log on to the Internet. Figure 9 shows the recent growth in the number of devices in the United States that can access the Web, while Figure 10 shows the corresponding increase in the number of Web pages. New users, and new providers of content, require Internet access, encouraging the creation of more ISPs, which in turn encourages the entry of more Internet backbone providers and fiber providers to transport the additional data. These ISPs compete to attract new users and content providers in a continuation of the virtuous cycle that has led to the unprecedented growth level that characterizes the Internet.

In recognition of the role of regulatory abstention in the development of the Internet, the 1996 Act states that "[t]he Internet … [has] flourished, to the benefit of all Americans, with a minimum of government regulation."[62] Yet the commercial backbone market is relatively young, and industry observers are questioning whether the government can, or should, maintain a fully hands-off approach to backbone providers. The next section shows how competition, hand-in-hand with antitrust laws and competition enforcement, can act to restrain any anti-competitive actions in place of industry-specific regulations.

III. Interconnection Issues

This section examines the market outcomes that result from unregulated interconnection agreements between backbone providers. There have been a number of allegations, discussed below, that the entire system of interconnection between backbones is at risk due to the actions of several larger backbones. At least one industry observer argued that the emerging system of private peering enables the larger backbones to act in an anti-competitive manner by excluding smaller backbones from private peering arrangements and then raising prices.[63] While universal connectivity is the norm today, as new real-time services begin to be offered over the Internet, there are fears that in the future backbones may choose to differentiate themselves by not interconnecting for purposes of offering these new services. The paper examines whether there

---

[61]   "With Series of Deals, PSINet seeks to become 'Super Carrier'," *Communications Daily*, Oct. 20, 1999.

[62]   Furthermore, "[it] is the policy of the United States to preserve the vibrant and competitive free market that presently exists for the Internet...." 47 U.S.C. § 230 (a)(4), (b)(2).

[63]   Jack Rickard, "Yet another unique moment in time. Peering redux – back to the future and the essentials of a competitive Internet," Editor's Notes, May 1998, *Boardwatch Magazine*.

is any possible market failure in the Internet backbone market that could not be governed adequately by existing antitrust laws.

A. Internet Backbone Market Power Issues

1. Background

Internet backbone providers face conflicting incentives. On one hand, they have an incentive to cooperate with one another in order to provide their customers with access to the full range of Internet users and content. On the other hand, these same backbones have an incentive to compete with one another for both retail and wholesale customers. The need for backbone A to interconnect with backbone B in order to provide its customers access to backbone B's customers creates what might be termed a *competitive network externality*; this interconnection also enables backbone B to provide its customers access to backbone A's customers. As long as A and B are relatively equally sized, there is a strong incentive for them to cooperate with one another in spite of competitive network externalities; if either unilaterally stops interconnecting, it has no guarantees that it will benefit from such an action. This situation seems to characterize the early days of the commercial Internet, when a number of backbones were relatively similar in size, and readily agreed to peer with one another. Recently, however, there have been allegations that as certain backbones grew they began to engage in uncooperative, if not anti-competitive, practices.[64]

In early 1997, UUNET, followed by several other large backbones, attempted to end peering with a number of smaller backbones and instead charge them for transit.[65] In another example, GTE Internetworking, since renamed Genuity, announced that it would no longer privately peer with Exodus Communications, as did PSINet more recently.[66] When WorldCom, which had purchased UUNET and several other backbones, announced a merger agreement with MCI, there was concern that the combined backbone would become the dominant backbone with the ability to exercise market power against smaller competitors in a variety of ways.[67] In particular, merger opponents argued that the merged firm would refuse to peer with smaller

---

[64] For instance, Level 3's Chairman, James Crowe, claimed that MCI and WorldCom's refusal to peer with Level 3 constituted "monopolistic behavior." Joan Engebretson, "Level 3: Whiner or Visionary," *Telephony Magazine*, May 25, 1998 at 7. *See also* John J. Keller, "Level 3 Assails the WorldCom-MCI Deal," *The Wall Street Journal*, May 20, 1998, at B10.

[65] Because interconnection agreements are generally confidential due to the widespread use of non-disclosure agreements, it is not commonly known whether this attempt was successful. *See id.*

[66] Kate Gerwig, "Service Providers Still in Peering Dither," *InternetWeek*, August 27, 1998, http://www.internetwk.com/news0898/news082798-2.htm. Martin Kady II, "Peer Pressure: Dissolution of PSINet, Exodus Network-Sharing Agreement May be Sign of Things to Come," *Washington Business Journal*, June 2-8, 2000 ("Peer Pressure") at 1.

[67] *See Application of WorldCom, Inc. and MCI Communications Corporation for Transfer of Control of MCI Communications Corporation to WorldCom, Inc.*, CC Docket No. 97-211, Memorandum Opinion and Order, 13 FCC Rcd 18025, 18103-18115, paras. 142-156 (1998)(*MCI/WorldCom Order*). In order to satisfy antitrust concerns regarding increased concentration in the Internet backbone market, MCI sold its Internet assets to Cable &Wireless. *See* European Commission Press Release, "Commission Clears WorldCom and MCI Merger Subject to Conditions," July 8, 1998 (European Commission MCI WorldCom Press Release); DOJ Press Release, "Justice Department Clears WorldCom/MCI Merger After MCI Agrees to Sell its Internet Business," July 15, 1998 (DOJ MCI WorldCom Press Release); *MCI/WorldCom Order*, 13 FCC Rcd at 18109-18115, paras. 151-156. The Federal Communications Commission did conclude, however, that "peering is likely to remain an issue that warrants monitoring." *Id.* at 18115, para. 155.

backbones. For instance, Level 3 argued that both MCI and WorldCom were refusing to peer with Level 3, and that the merger would increase the merger partners' incentives to discriminate against rivals seeking to interconnect.[68] These concerns were echoed in the recent MCI WorldCom/Sprint merger proceeding.[69] During this proceeding, Level 3 argued that Sprint was refusing to peer with Level 3, a refusal that "cannot be explained by competitive market forces."[70] Likewise, when Exodus was refused peering by PSINet, Adam Wegner, general counsel for Exodus stated that "[Exodus] view[s] [PSINet's] action as anti-competitive."[71]

This section considers whether a backbone's refusal to peer with another backbone is likely to be anti-competitive. Anti-competitive is defined to mean the ability of a firm (or firms) to maintain prices profitably above the level that would otherwise result from a competitive market. The search for anti-competitive actions focuses on actions that harm consumers, but do not necessarily harm competitors, for actions that harm competitors may not in fact harm consumers.[72] For instance, a merger may increase the efficiency of a firm and result in lower retail prices. While this may harm competitors, if many rivals remain in the market the merger is not anti-competitive, because lower prices benefit consumers. If a market failure is found that leads to anti-competitive actions on the part of one or more Internet backbone providers, a determination must then be made whether antitrust laws would provide a sufficient remedy, or if industry-specific regulation is required.

The effect of a backbone's refusing to peer with another backbone depends on the degree of competition in the backbone market. In a competitive market, a backbone may refuse to peer with a smaller rival for legitimate, rather than anti-competitive, reasons.[73] The paper shows that, in a competitive market, backbones that have been denied peering can nevertheless enter the backbone market, because competition among the larger top-tier backbones gives them an incentive to provide transit arrangements to smaller backbones in place of peering. If, on the other hand, there was a dominant backbone, the dominant backbone might be able to disadvantage actual or potential rivals in an anti-competitive manner by, for instance, not peering or not providing transit to smaller backbones.

---

[68] *See* Letter from Terrence J. Ferguson, Senior Vice President and General Counsel, Level 3 Communications, to Magalie Roman Salas, Secretary, FCC, Attach. (filed May 29, 1998 in CC Docket No. 97-211, *Application of WorldCom, Inc. and MCI Communications Corporation for Transfer of Control of MCI Communications Corporation to WorldCom, Inc.*) (Level 3 May 29 1998, *Ex Parte*).

[69] DOJ WorldCom Sprint Complaint, pp. 14-21.

[70] Reply Comments of Level 3 Communications, at 11 (filed March 20, 2000 in CC Docket No. 99-333, *Application for Consent to the Transfer of Control of Licenses from Sprint Corporation to MCI WorldCom, Inc.*).

[71] Martin Kady II, "Peer Pressure," at 3.

[72] *See, e.g., Continental T.V., Inc. v. GTE Sylvania Inc.*, 433 U.S. 36, 59 (1977).

[73] Here we focus on reasons to deny peering that have their roots in economic considerations. Peering may also be denied for technical reasons, as a peer could be exposed to significant harms resulting from errors on the part of peering partners. A backbone with little technical competence may find willing peering partners scarce for technical reasons alone.

2. Analysis

a) Competitive Backbone Market

An important determinant of the competitiveness of any market is whether new firms can enter the market, and smaller firms can expand, thereby constraining any potential exercise of market power by the existing larger firms. In order to enter or expand, Internet backbones need to interconnect with existing backbones in order to enable their customers to exchange traffic with the customers of existing firms, and they need access to fiber capacity to carry their traffic. As described above, fiber capacity is readily available, and thus this section will focus on the ability of smaller Internet backbones to interconnect with larger ones. Much of the current debate focuses on the effects of one backbone refusing to peer with another backbone. This paper attempts to inform such discussions by showing that, in a competitive backbone market, there may be a number of legitimate reasons for one backbone to refuse to peer with another backbone. Therefore, such a refusal may not constitute a barrier to entering the backbone market. As long as transit arrangements are available on a competitive basis, smaller backbones can enter and ensure that the backbone market remains competitive.

One reason a backbone may refuse to peer is that it believes that peering would enable the other backbone to free ride on its infrastructure investments. Figure 6 illustrates this situation. In the figure, backbone *B*, a national backbone, has a presence on both coasts. Backbone *A*, in contrast, is a regional backbone with a presence only on the East coast. If the two backbones peered on the East coast, when a customer of backbone *A* requests a web page from a customer of backbone *B* whose server is on the West coast, then backbone *B* would carry the request from the East coast to the West coast and also carry the response back to the East coast. The national backbone may thus refuse to peer on the grounds that it would otherwise bear the expense for a national infrastructure from which the regional carrier could then benefit at no cost. As a result of such considerations, a number of backbones require that peering partners be willing and able to interconnect at a number of geographically diverse locations.[74] This consideration seems to have motivated UUNET's decision to change its peering policy in 1997.[75]

---

[74] For instance, UUNET's North American Peering Policy states, among other things, that "a peering candidate needs to meet UUNET at minimally four geographically diverse locations across the US," with a minimum requirement of an East coast location and a West coast location, with, "ideally" two Midwest locations. The stated intention is "to minimize the backhaul of traffic across both networks." Letter from Valerie Yates, counsel, MCI WorldCom, to Magalie R. Salas, Secretary, FCC, Attach., (filed April 13, 2000 in CC Docket No. 99-333, *Application for Consent to the Transfer of Control of Licenses from Sprint Corporation to MCI WorldCom, Inc.*)(UUNET Peering Policy). Sprint's Bi-Lateral Peering Policy contains a similar provision, that peering partners must be able to support peering arrangements "at 4 geographically diverse domestic U.S. locations." Letter from Michael G. Jones, counsel, Sprint, to Magalie R. Salas, Secretary, FCC, Attach., (filed April 13, 2000 in CC Docket No. 99-333, *Application for Consent to the Transfer of Control of Licenses from Sprint Corporation to MCI WorldCom, Inc.*)(Sprint Peering Policy). Finally, Genuity recently published its Internet Interconnect Guidelines. Genuity Press Release, "Genuity Announces Public Posting of Interconnect Guidelines," September 8, 2000. One of the criteria for public peering with Genuity is a presence at three or more Shared Interconnection Points (NAPs) where Genuity has a presence, two of which must be MAE-East and MAE-West. "Internet Interconnection Guidelines for Genuity," http://www.genuity.com/infrastructure/interconnection.htm (Genuity Interconnection Guidelines).

[75] At the time, the president and CEO of UUNET, John Sidgmore, argued that "a few years ago all ISPs were generally the same size and used each other's infrastructures to a more or less equal extent… that situation no longer

The "hot-potato routing" that characterizes peering arrangements may also lead to actual or perceived free-riding, as a result of the decision on the part of some backbones to specialize in providing service mainly to one type of customer, such as content providers. This situation can be illustrated by referring back to Figure 5. Suppose that ISP Y, a customer of backbone B, provides service mainly to content providers, while ISP X, a customer of backbone A, provides service mainly to end users. Given hot-potato routing, when a end user customer of ISP X requests content that is hosted by ISP Y, backbone B will carry the request from the East coast to the West coast, while backbone A would carry the requested content back from the West coast. As a rule, content such as Web pages involve more bits of data than the corresponding requests for the content. Therefore, backbones such as A that carry the Web pages would transport more traffic than would backbones such as B that carry the requests for these Web pages. Backbones may thus refuse to peer with backbones hosting a high proportion of content providers on the grounds that they are bearing the expense for more capacity than the backbone that is actually hosting the content that utilizes this capacity.[76] This consideration may have motivated GTE Internetworking (now Genuity) and PSINet to refuse to peer with Exodus, a company that provides network services to content providers.[77]

The preceding paragraphs show that, in order to prevent free-riding, a large backbone may refuse to peer with a smaller backbone. In a competitive market, these refusals may not have any anti-competitive intent or effect; indeed, such refusals may in fact have a pro-competitive result. A smaller backbone, denied peering on the grounds of free-riding, may then have an incentive to invest in infrastructure and compete for a varied mix of new customers in order to qualify for peering – resulting in an increased number of competing national backbone providers. As discussed below, this is only possible as long as a smaller backbone that has been denied peering is able to enter the market with a transit relationship.

The next example examines the situation of a backbone that is refused peering because it has a small customer base. There are indications that a backbone may refuse to peer with a smaller backbone based on the amount of traffic generated by the smaller backbone. For instance, the published peering policies of UUNET, Sprint, and Genuity all contain a requirement that a peering candidate be able to exchange a certain minimum amount of data at the beginning of the peering relationship.[78] An MCI spokesperson was quoted as saying that, for

exists and consequently there are many cases where peering is not appropriate." UUNET Press Release, "UUNET Details Peering Strategy," May 12, 1997, http://www.us.uu.net/press/1997/peering.shtml (UUNET May 12, 1997 Press Release).

[76]   UUNET, for one, argues that companies that provide "web server farm" services and request peering with UUNET are "seeking to use UUNET's network for free, after UUNET has spent hundreds of millions of dollars to create its infrastructure." *Id.*

[77]   John Curran, then Chief Technical Officer of GTE Internetworking, was quoted as saying that the traffic exchange with Exodus was "'wildly asymmetrical,'" and that as a result Exodus was getting a free ride from GTE Internetworking. Genuity now specifically states in its Internet Interconnection Guidelines that one of the criteria for traffic exchange with Genuity is, "[f]or domestic ISPs, roughly balanced traffic." Genuity Interconnection Guidelines. Kate Gerwig, "Service Providers." Similarly, Bob Leahy, Vice President of Marketing for PSINet, stated of Exodus that "[w]e were tired of carrying their load. They are a pure hosting play. What makes them meritorious to get free peering?" Martin Kady II, "Peer Pressure."

[78]   UUNET expects a peering candidate "to exchange at least 40 Megabits of traffic total average utilization." UUNET Peering Policy. Sprint's peering policy has a provision that the "average monthly traffic exchange between Sprint and the peering network must be justifiable." Sprint Peering Policy. One of the criteria for traffic exchange

this reason, Level 3 was denied peering by MCI.[79] One justification given by the larger backbones is that it is difficult and costly to allocate necessary resources to potential peers with low current volumes that may or may not grow rapidly in the future. Nevertheless, this requirement may place backbones with low volumes in a Catch-22 situation; without a large number of customers generating traffic volume, it is not possible to negotiate peering arrangements with the large backbones, yet without peering, it may be difficult to gain the large number of customers necessary to generate the traffic volume to qualify for peering. In order to determine whether the latter statement is valid, one must examine the implications for smaller backbones of not being able to peer with larger backbones.

It is important to differentiate between larger backbones refusing to *interconnect* with smaller backbones, versus the larger backbones only refusing to *peer* with smaller backbones. Instead of peering with the smaller backbones, the larger backbones may offer them a transit arrangement.[80] For instance, if backbone *A* is refused peering by backbone *B*, then backbone *A* could use a transit arrangement in order for its customers to have access to backbone *B*'s customers. Backbone *A* could take transit directly from backbone *B*, or it could become a transit customer of a third backbone *C* that is interconnected with backbone *B,* as in Figure 4. The paper first argues that in a competitive market, larger backbones that refuse to peer have an incentive to offer smaller backbones transit, and then shows that transit is likely to be offered on a competitive basis.

Having denied peering to smaller backbones, one might question whether the larger top-tier backbones providing transit would either refuse to provide transit to smaller backbones or simply increase the cost of transit in order to squeeze out the smaller rivals. There are two reasons that this would be unlikely in a competitive backbone market. The first reason is unique to the Internet. In negotiating peering, one important bargaining chip is the number of customers to which a backbone provides access; this includes the number of transit customers. Therefore, backbones will compete with each other to win transit customers to use as leverage when negotiating peering relationships with other backbones. The second reason is traditional, that the large backbones will compete for the transit business of smaller backbones in order to increase their revenues, which will keep transit prices down. In a growing market such as the Internet market, in particular, one would not expect it to be profitable for a competitive backbone to raise price, and thereby restrict sales, and growth in sales. Therefore, in a competitive backbone market, no backbone provider is likely to find it profitable to use a price squeeze to disadvantage smaller rivals.

As a transit customer, it may be possible for a smaller backbone provider to grow and later qualify to peer with backbones that initially refused peering, including the transit supplier. Nevertheless, a smaller backbone may prefer peering rather then being a paying transit customer, either for quality or cost reasons. The paper next examines whether, in a competitive market, a

---

with Genuity is a "minimum Internet traffic exchange of 1 Mbps with Autonomous System 1." Genuity Interconnection Guidelines.

[79]   Joan Engebretson, "Level 3: Whiner or Visionary?"

[80]   *See, e.g.,* Rob Frieden, "Without Public Peer: The Potential Regulatory and Universal Service Consequences of Internet Balkanization," *Virginia Journal of Law and Technology,* Fall 1998, Vol. 3, No. 8, ("Without Public Peer") at 1522-1687, para. 16.

smaller backbone that only interconnects via a transit arrangement is likely to be at a competitive disadvantage.

Because transit does not involve the same service as peering, refusing peering in favor of transit is not simply a means of charging for a service that was otherwise provided free of charge. In a transit relationship, one backbone must pay another for access to the Internet. For instance, at the time that UUNET changed its peering policy in 1997, it announced that wholesale connectivity started at $2,000 per month for a T-1 connection and $6,000 for a fractional T-3 connection.[81] Transit customers receive benefits in return for these payments; when backbones pay for transit they benefit from the infrastructure investments of national or global backbones without themselves having to make or utilize their own investments. In addition, as noted above, transit gives a backbone access to the entire Internet, not just the customers of the peering partner. In order to provide transit customers with access to the entire Internet, the transit provider must either maintain peering arrangements with a number of other backbones or in turn must pay for transit from yet another backbone. In other words, a backbone providing transit services is providing access to a greater array of end users and content than it would as a peer, thereby incurring correspondingly higher costs that are recuperated in the transit payments. In a competitive backbone market, transit prices should reflect costs and should not put entering backbones at a competitive disadvantage.

In terms of the quality of transit, Level 3 has suggested that, as a transit customer of another backbone, Level 3 would depend on the supplying backbone for delivery of IP traffic, at the very least placing Level 3 at a marketing disadvantage.[82] This view was affirmed in the DOJ Complaint in the MCI WorldCom/Sprint merger proceeding.[83] Nevertheless, at least one backbone, SAVVIS, initially relied only on transit connections and not peering, and was very competitive in terms of quality.[84] Quality may improve with transit, at least compared with public peering at a NAP, because a transit connection may avoid the congestion of passing through a NAP to get access to a backbone. According to an executive at Digex, a Web-hosting company that used to own its own backbone, "[w]ith free peering, the level of service is not as good. It costs more [to pay for access], but the quality of service is better."[85] In sum, there is evidence that paying for transit does not put a transit customer at an insurmountable disadvantage from a quality point of view.

---

[81]   UUNET May 12, 1997 Press Release. A T-1 connection is a digital transmission link with a capacity of 1.544 Mbps. A fractional T-3 connection is a portion of a T-3 (44.7364 Mbps) digital transmission link. Letter from Terrence J. Ferguson, Senior Vice President and General Counsel, Level 3 Communications, to Michelle Carey, Common Carrier Bureau, FCC, (filed August 7, 1998 in CC Docket No. 97-211, *Application of WorldCom, Inc. and MCI Communications Corporation for Transfer of Control of MCI Communications Corporation to WorldCom, Inc.*) (Level 3 Aug. 7 1998, *Ex Parte*), Attach. at 4.

[82]   Level 3 May 29 1998, *Ex Parte* at 4.

[83]   DOJ WorldCom Sprint Complaint at 13.

[84]   Doug Mohney, "SAVVIS Shifts Gears and Ownership," *Boardwatch*, April 1999. <http://boardwatch.internet.com/mag/99/apr/bwm66.html>. In 1997, SAVVIS Internet was rated the highest quality backbone provider by Keynote Systems. Jack Rickard, Editor's Notes, *Boardwatch Magazine*, May 1998. At the time, SAVVIS created private NAPs, bought transit from the largest backbones, and didn't peer at all, though Rickard notes that this is expensive.

[85]   Martin Kady II, "Peer Pressure," at 3, quoting Bobby Patrick, Vice President of Strategy at Digex.

In conclusion, the presence of a large number of top-tier backbones can prevent any anti-competitive actions. In a competitive backbone market, no large backbone would unilaterally end peering with another, as it has no guarantee that it will benefit from such an action. Furthermore, there would be no insurmountable barrier to entry or growth of smaller backbones. Larger top-tier backbones would continue to compete to provide transit services to smaller backbones. These smaller backbones would be able to resell these services to their own customers, and would not seem to face any barrier to acquiring either the infrastructure or customer base that could enable them eventually to join the ranks of the larger backbones and qualify for peering. Actual, as well as potential, entry by new backbones would act to constrain the actions of larger incumbent backbones, keeping prices at competitive levels.

b) Backbone Market with a Dominant Firm

If, on the other hand, a single backbone were dominant, it would be able to harm the public interest by engaging in a number of anti-competitive actions. As discussed above, it appears unlikely that a firm may organically grow to become dominant. Instead, the route to such dominance would likely be achieved by consolidation between backbone providers, or if a backbone gained market power over a key bottleneck input, such as transmission facilities. The issue of consolidation was at the heart of the debate surrounding WorldCom's acquisition of MCI, and later MCI WorldCom's acquisition of Sprint.[86] This section discusses the potential anti-competitive harms that could be caused by a dominant backbone. Many of these harms were raised by commenters in the MCI/WorldCom merger proceeding, and identified in the Commission's *MCI/WorldCom Order*.[87]

A dominant backbone could harm the public interest in a number of ways. First, by definition a dominant firm has the unilateral ability to profitably raise and sustain retail prices above competitive levels. In addition, a dominant backbone would have both the ability and the incentive to stop cooperating with smaller backbones. Failure to cooperate could take a number of forms, including refusing to interconnect at all, executing a price squeeze, or degrading the quality of interconnection by not upgrading the capacity of connections with smaller backbones.

A dominant backbone also could abuse market power by refusing to interconnect with smaller backbones. The network externalities literature has shown that, in general, a larger network has less of an incentive to become compatible or interconnect with a smaller network, as customers of the smaller network have more to gain from being able to communicate with customers of the larger network than vice versa.[88] In the context of the Internet, if a dominant backbone refused to interconnect with a smaller one, the customers of the smaller backbone

---

[86]   The issue of backbone consolidation during the MCI/WorldCom merger proceeding was resolved when MCI divested its Internet business to Cable & Wireless. *See supra* at *n.* 67. Later, as a result of the backbone consolidation, as well as other concerns, both the European Commission and the Department of Justice acted to block the MCI WorldCom/Sprint merger. *See* "Justice Department Sues to Block WorldCom's Acquisition of Sprint," Department of Justice Press Release, June 27, 2000; "Commission prohibits merger between MCI WorldCom and Sprint," European Commission Press Release, June 28, 2000 (European Commission WorldCom Sprint Press Release).

[87]   *MCI/WorldCom Order*, 13 FCC Rcd at paras. 149-150. Similar issues were raised by the Department of Justice in the course of the MCI WorldCom Sprint proceeding. *See* DOJ WorldCom Sprint Complaint at n. 93.

[88]   Katz and Shapiro, "Network Externalities;" Jacques Cremer, Patrick Rey, and Jean Tirole, "Connectivity in the Commercial Internet," May 1999, mimeo ("Connectivity").

would have an incentive to switch to the larger network in order to enjoy the network externalities associated with the larger backbone's customer base. Although customers of the dominant backbone would also lose access to the smaller network's customer base, they are unlikely to respond by switching to the smaller network. As a result, the smaller backbone would be positioned poorly to compete for customers, reinforcing the dominance of the largest backbone. It is noteworthy that the advantage of dominant networks also characterizes local telephony, where incumbent LECs must be compelled by statute to interconnect with smaller competitive LECs.[89]

A dominant backbone could also exercise market power by executing a price squeeze on those smaller backbones with which it interconnects. In a price squeeze situation, a vertically integrated firm with market power over an essential upstream input raises the price of this input to rivals competing in downstream retail markets. The increased cost of this essential input forces downstream rivals to raise their retail prices. The vertically integrated firm is then in a position to undercut the downstream rivals in retail markets and thereby increase market share and profits. In the backbone example, interconnection is the essential input that smaller backbones must have from the dominant backbone in order to compete with the dominant backbone to sell backbone services to ISPs or directly to end users. Dominant backbones can refuse to peer with smaller backbones, and also raise the price of transit services charged to those same backbones. This will weaken existing rivals, and also prevent the entry of new backbones. As a result, the dominant backbone can raise downstream prices and increase profits.

A dominant backbone also might engage in non-price discrimination against rival backbones.[90] During the MCI/WorldCom merger proceeding, GTE presented a scenario in which a dominant backbone might degrade interconnections with other backbones in order to win customers from those backbone providers. This could most easily be done by "slow rolling" necessary increases in the capacity of the trunks used to interconnect with other backbones. Such capacity increases are a regular necessity to keep pace with the rapid growth in demand for Internet services. Under this scheme, a backbone, A, may degrade a connection with a smaller backbone, B. As B's customers begin to feel the effects of this degradation when communicating with customers of backbone A, they may switch to backbone A in order to improve connections with customers of backbone A. It should be noted that, with two-way interconnections, the customers of backbone A would also be affected by this degradation when they attempt to communicate with the customers of backbone B. For this reason, A must be significantly larger than B so that its customers are relatively less adversely affected than the customers of B and do not themselves switch.[91] In order to limit further the effects of non-price discrimination on its own customers, GTE argued that backbone A would engage in what it called "serial degradation" and target only one smaller backbone at a time.

This section shows that, if a backbone were to become dominant, it could act in an anti-competitive fashion. Such a backbone market would share many characteristics with other network industries that traditionally warranted regulation, and it might then be in the public

---

[89]   See 47 U.S.C. § 251.

[90]   See Cremer, Rey, and Tirole, "Connectivity." These authors advised GTE on the non-price discrimination issue during the MCI WorldCom proceeding, and formalized their analysis in that paper.

[91]   GTE and its experts note that in a situation in which there is no dominant backbone, there would be no incentive for any backbone to attempt a serial degradation strategy in order to become dominant. *Id.*, Section 6.

interest to apply similar regulations to the backbone market. The paper shows above that, conversely, as long as there are a number of competing top-tier backbone providers, entry is possible. In that case, there would be no need for any change in the current unregulated status of the Internet. The next section shows that, although competition between backbone providers is unregulated, consumers nevertheless benefit from the same protections afforded consumers of all products and services. Existing antitrust policies, as applied in the MCI/WorldCom and MCI WorldCom/Sprint merger proceedings by the Department of Justice and the European Commission, along with the Federal Communications Commission's application of the public interest standard in the MCI/WorldCom case, can prevent the emergence of a dominant backbone in an otherwise competitive market.[92]

3. Consumer Protection in the Backbone Market

This paper has already discussed the underpinnings of the industry-specific regulation of network industries – when the underlying cost structure of an industry does not support competition, it may be in the public interest to regulate the prices and services offered by the resulting natural monopoly. There are only a select few network industries in the United States for which market failures have been considered severe enough that regulations have been imposed to govern prices and service quality on an ongoing basis. Where competition is possible, regulation may be relaxed or eliminated, to the extent that market forces can govern prices and services in place of regulations. Even where competition is possible, however, it is not guaranteed. As a result, antitrust laws have been enacted to protect consumers from anti-competitive behavior by a firm (or firms) that seek to acquire or exploit market power. The antitrust laws apply to the Internet backbone as they do to every other product and service market, and indeed they already have been invoked in the cases of the MCI/WorldCom and MCI WorldCom/Sprint mergers. Many of the above arguments about the potential actions of a dominant backbone were raised during these merger proceedings.[93] These proceedings showed that the combined efforts of the European Commission and the Department of Justice, enforcing relevant antitrust statutes, as well as the Commission itself, upholding the public interest standard, can prevent an increase in the concentration of the backbone market that could threaten consumer welfare.[94]

In the MCI/WorldCom merger proceeding, MCI divested its Internet business to Cable & Wireless in order to eliminate any overlap between MCI and WorldCom in the Internet backbone market, and thereby satisfied concerns expressed by the Department of Justice and the European Union.[95] Parties argued at the time, however, that the degree to which MCI's Internet business was integrated with its other business units might complicate such a divestiture, in comparison with the divestiture of a standalone business unit such as WorldCom's UUNET backbone.[96] All relevant agencies approved the transaction based on their conclusion that the terms of the divestiture contract adequately addressed any potential complications arising from the divestiture

---

[92]   *See MCI/WorldCom Order*, 13 FCC Rcd at paras. 8-14.

[93]   *See, e.g.*, DOJ WorldCom Sprint Complaint at 9-21.

[94]   *See supra* at n. 35.

[95]   *See supra* at n. 67.

[96]   *See* Reuters English News Service, "C&W seen urging EU to be tough on MCI, Sprint Buy," November 29, 1999. *See also MCI/WorldCom Order*, 13 FCC Rcd at 18109-18115, paras. 151-156.

of an integrated unit such as MCI's Internet business.[97] Since the divestiture, however, Cable & Wireless filed suit against MCI, claiming that MCI breached the divestiture contract by not transferring its complete Internet business; according to Mike McTighe, Chief Executive Officer of Cable & Wireless Global Operations, "MCI WorldCom's material breaches of the [divestiture] Undertakings threaten to impair Cable & Wireless's competitiveness."[98] This suit, which was settled, shows that the details of a divestiture may be important.[99] A complete divestiture of a business unit by one of the merging firms may mean that the market share of the merged entity does not change as a result of the merger. However, the competitive landscape may nevertheless change if the divested unit is harmed as a result of the divestiture, and therefore poses less of a competitive constraint to the merged firm.[100]

In addition to horizontal concentration in the backbone market, vertical integration could also lead to market power. Backbones may vertically integrate upstream into the market for the telecommunications inputs that underlie the services that backbones provide. Indeed, many backbones, such as WorldCom and Sprint, are already vertically integrated, owning their own fiber optic networks. Because telecommunications transport capacity is readily available today from a wide variety of providers, including the vertically integrated backbones themselves, vertical integration itself is unlikely to create a barrier to entry. As with mergers of backbones, antitrust laws, and specifically merger policy, should prevent undue consolidation of the telecommunications transport market that could lead the remaining telecommunications providers to engage in anti-competitive actions in the downstream Internet backbone market. In addition, existing common carrier regulations prevent vertically integrated telecommunications carriers from refusing to provide any necessary upstream telecommunications services sought by competing backbone providers.

There also may be concern about downstream relationships between backbones and the Internet service providers for whom backbone services are a vital input. In addition to vertical integration, backbone providers could enter into exclusive dealing arrangements with ISPs, such that the backbone provider would provide only one ISP with its services. Likewise, backbones that already are vertically integrated with ISPs could choose to not provide backbone services to unaffiliated ISPs. In the growing Internet market, such an exclusionary arrangement is unlikely, however, because backbones have incentives to increase the number of customers that they have as bargaining chips in peering negotiations. In addition, given the availability of telecommunications inputs and transit arrangements, the possibilities of entry into either the ISP market or the backbone market could not be foreclosed by such a vertical arrangement.

---

[97] *Id. See also* European Union MCI/WorldCom Press Release; DOJ MCI/WorldCom Press Release.

[98] Testimony of Mike McTighe before the United States Senate Commerce Committee, Telecommunications mergers hearing, November 8, 1999. *See also* Denise Pappalardo, "Did Cable & Wireless Get the Shaft?", *Network World*, April 5, 1999.

[99] "MCI WorldCom and Cable & Wireless Reach Agreement over Internet Dispute," Cable & Wireless Press Release, March 1, 2000 ("MCI WorldCom has agreed to pay Cable & Wireless $200 million in full and final settlement of the disputes.").

[100] In the recent MCI WorldCom/Sprint merger proceeding, the European Commission found the merging parties' proposal to divest Sprint's Internet business insufficient, concluding that the divested business would not "become a strong, viable competitor to prevent the merged WorldCom/Sprint from dominating Internet backbone." The European Commission noted that it explicitly took into account the issues raised by Cable & Wireless after its purchase of MCI's Internet assets. European Commission WorldCom/Sprint Press Release.

Thus, the lack of industry-specific regulation of Internet backbones does not expose consumers to economic risks that are different than those faced by consumers of other, non-network products and services. Internet markets are subject to the same antitrust regulations that act to govern other industries in the event that competition is no longer able to provide customers with just and reasonable prices and quality levels.

The sections above show how, in a competitive environment without a dominant firm, interconnection, either by transit or peering, will be available to existing and new backbones. While consolidation is the most obvious means for a backbone to become dominant, as discussed above, there are other means by which a backbone could grow to become dominant. For example, one way is for a provider to leverage market power over last-mile access to end users into market power in the backbone market – an important issue that is best left to an analysis of the market for last- mile access. In another scenario, a new or existing backbone could develop a proprietary technology that makes it either more efficient or more attractive to end-user customers. If this technology is a new service, for example, the backbone may choose not to interconnect with other backbones for the provision of this new service. As customers switch to this backbone in order to benefit from the new service, the backbone may grow to become dominant.

If a dominant backbone provider were to emerge, this backbone provider could engage in a variety of anti-competitive actions, as described above, that would ultimately harm consumers. In this case, industry-specific regulation of the dominant backbone provider may be in the public interest. Other network industries such as telephony also have warranted industry-specific regulation, and the resulting regulations may provide a template for the regulations that could be imposed on a dominant backbone provider. Such regulations could include, for instance, interconnection obligations that would govern the peering and transit relationships offered by the dominant backbone provider. Any regulation of the Internet backbone market would represent a significant shift in the unregulated status quo under which the Internet industry has grown at unprecedented rates, and therefore would require a corresponding significant shift in the competitiveness of the market.

B. Internet Balkanization Issues

Although it may be unlikely that any backbone is able to gain sufficient market power so as to be able to act in an anti-competitive fashion, today's environment of universal connectivity among backbones nevertheless may not be stable in the long run. Firms in all markets attempt to differentiate their products from other companies for one or more of the following reasons: to help attract new customers; to increase their hold over existing customers; or to be able to profitably raise retail prices. Internet backbones may thus attempt to differentiate themselves from each other by offering certain new or existing services only to their own customers. As a result, the Internet may "balkanize," with competing backbones not interconnecting to provide all services.[101] This may resemble the early days of telephony, when not all local companies were interconnected.

---

[101] *See* Frieden "Without Public Peer." Professor Frieden raises issues similar to the ones dealt with in this paper, with a focus on the effects of such balkanization on universal access to the Internet, notably in rural areas.

The dynamic nature of the Internet means that today's market structure and relationships likely will change. New services are continually being made available over the Internet. Many of these services, including Internet telephony and video-conferencing, are real-time applications that are sensitive to any delays in transmission. As a result, quality of service (QoS) is becoming a critical issue for backbones and ISPs. The paper considers whether or not two backbones would establish high-quality interconnections over which they could guarantee QoS levels to their customers wishing to communicate in real-time with customers of the other backbone.[102] The paper focuses on the economics behind a decision to interconnect to guarantee QoS, while assuming that any technical barriers to such interconnection could be overcome.[103] Backbones face a number of private economic considerations in making such interconnection decisions. Any private decision by one or more backbones not to interconnect to guarantee QoS levels for new services may also have public consequences, however, as consumers of one backbone may not be able to use these new services to communicate with consumers of another backbone. The paper shows that there are strong market forces that would lead firms to interconnect in order to exchange traffic originating from these new services. If such interconnection does not materialize, proponents of any industry-specific interconnection regulation should nevertheless show why the lack of such interconnection justifies regulatory intervention.

The decision to interconnect for the provision of QoS services would appear to be relatively similar to the one that backbones currently make when deciding whether to peer with one another. The backbones each calculate whether the benefits of interconnecting with one or more other backbones would outweigh the costs. The benefits of interconnecting to exchange traffic flow from increasing the network of customers with whom one can communicate; this helps attract new users, and encourages usage from existing users. The cost comes from a competitive network externality, as defined above; one backbone's decision to interconnect with another backbone makes the other backbone more attractive to customers. The widespread interconnection available today, in the form of either peering or transit agreements, indicates that currently, the benefits of interconnection outweigh any costs.

There is, however, a difference between current interconnection arrangements and new interconnection arrangements for the exchange of QoS traffic. The Internet services that interconnection enables today, such as email and Web access, already are universally available, and no one backbone or ISP could differentiate itself based on its unique provision of these services. Universal connectivity, however, is a legacy of the cooperative spirit that characterized the Internet in its early days. In the commercial spirit that pervades the Internet today, backbones and ISPs may view the new services that rely on QoS as a means to differentiate themselves from their competitors. A firm that introduces these new services may be less willing to share the ability to provide these services with competitors, as such sharing may reduce the ability of the firm to charge a premium to its own customers. For instance, UUNET announced a Service Level Agreement (SLA) that guarantees, among other things, the delivery speed (latency) of customers' traffic on its network.[104] This guarantee does not extend to traffic that leaves UUNET's network, however, which encourages customers to keep traffic on-net.

---

[102] *See also* Michael Kende and Douglas C. Sicker, "Slice and Dice: The Fragmentation of the Internet," Draft Paper, 2000.

[103] *See* Douglas C. Sicker, Joshua Mindel, and Cameron Cooper, "The Internet Interconnection Conundrum," OPP Working Paper (publication pending), 2000.

[104] *See* http://www.uunet.com.

Even if backbones agree in principle to interconnect in order to be able to offer new services that require QoS guarantees, they may face practical difficulties in reaching a final interconnection agreement. Aside from disagreements over the terms of interconnection, it is possible that the backbones, or their ISP customers, must support compatible versions of a particular new service in order to be able to exchange traffic that originates with one backbone's end user and terminates with another backbone's end user. Before committing to a particular standard for this service, backbones may wish to wait for an industry-wide standard to emerge. This presents a coordination problem that may be difficult to resolve – in particular, if any firms have developed their own proprietary standards that they wish to see adopted as the industry-wide standard. In this situation, in spite of the fact that backbones would be willing to interconnect to exchange QoS traffic, the end result may be the same as if they were not willing to interconnect – end users would not be able to communicate across backbones using certain services.

Another potential issue relating to interconnection for QoS services is that it may exacerbate current congestion, and therefore it may be difficult to guarantee QoS across backbones. Assuming that interconnection for QoS traffic is implemented under the current settlement-free peering system, backbones will not be paid to terminate QoS traffic. As a result, receiving backbones will have little or no economic incentive to increase capacity to terminate this traffic. QoS traffic that traverses networks may thus face congestion and would be unlikely to provide satisfactory quality. Of course, similar problems exist today with the current peering system, as described above, leading to the current congestion, but given the high data volume characterizing such services, the problem may be worsened. In order to provide the proper economic incentives to be able to guarantee to customers that they can deliver QoS traffic across networks, backbones may have to implement a traffic-sensitive settlement system for such traffic.[105]

If backbones are unable to overcome the economic, administrative, and technical hurdles to interconnect to exchange traffic flowing from new services requiring QoS, then the Internet faces the risk of balkanization. Backbones will only provide certain new services for use among their own customers. The result would be that network externalities, once taken for granted, would suddenly play a major role for consumers of Internet services. In the current environment of universal connectivity, consumers who simply want to send and receive email and surf on the Web can choose any retail provider without worrying about the choices of other consumers or content providers. If the Internet balkanizes over the offering of new services, consumers would need to be aware of the choices of those with whom they wish to communicate when making their own choice of Internet provider. For instance, a consumer who wishes to view real-time

---

[105]   Settlements are payments from a carrier that originates traffic to another carrier for terminating this traffic. A form of settlement exists in local and international telephony today. In local telephony, the settlement system is known as reciprocal compensation. Although reciprocal compensation can take the form of bill-and-keep, which is similar to peering, this is seldom the case. International settlements are governed by the bilateral accounting rate system. A settlement system for the Internet would enable backbones to recoup the costs associated with terminating QoS traffic that originated on other backbones, giving backbones the proper incentive to invest in the capacity necessary to guarantee the timely delivery of this traffic. The technical and administrative costs of implementing such a system on the Internet are formidable, however. *See, e.g.*, Maria Farnon and Scott Huddle, "Settlement Systems for the Internet," in Brian Kahin and James H. Keller, eds., *Coordinating the Internet* (MIT Press, 1997) at 377-403.

streaming video may need to be sure that the provider is connected to the same backbone to ensure high quality viewing. Likewise, a business that wishes to use the Internet for videoconferencing must make sure that all relevant branches, customers, and suppliers are connected to the same backbone. Thus any balkanization of the Internet would result in a classic example of network externalities; the specific backbone choice of each consumer would influence the choices of other consumers.

As a result of any balkanization of the Internet with respect to the provision of new services, customers wishing to communicate with a wide variety of others may end up subscribing to competing backbones, unless customers can coordinate on the choice of one backbone. This would raise the specter of the early days of telephony, when competing telephone companies refused to interconnect, resulting in many businesses and even some homes owning more than one telephone, corresponding to multiple local telephone company subscriptions.[106] As with the telephone system before it, any Internet balkanization may lead to calls for some form of interconnection regulation for backbones. This paper argues that such regulations are unlikely to be necessary.

It is important to reiterate that network industries such as telephony, water, and electricity, have historically been regulated based on their cost structure, to prevent a natural monopoly from exploiting customers. Such network industries are not generally regulated solely to provide customers the demand-side network externalities described above.[107] To impose interconnection regulations on Internet backbone providers in order to increase the benefits from network externalities for new services would represent a break from regulatory tradition.

There are many examples of products like the Internet that provide both direct and indirect network externalities that are not subject to industry-specific regulations. For instance, almost every consumer electronics product consists of a hardware/software system with indirect network externalities. The usefulness of compact disk players, personal computers, web browsers, and videocassette recorders depends to a great degree, if not totally, on the availability of compatible "software." The greater the number of users of the relevant "hardware," the more software will be available. Likewise, fax machines and email involve direct communications between end users with corresponding direct network externalities. In all of these cases, the market set the adopted standards, or ensured that various companies' products were compatible with one another, without any government intervention.

The marketplace has been quite successful at choosing standards that allow the products and services of different companies to be compatible with one another. Often, this is accomplished by a standards battle, such as the one waged between Betamax and VHS for the videocassette recorder standard. In other cases, one firm may create an adapter that enables its

---

[106] As an example of this phenomenon, in 1910, Louisville, Kentucky was served by two local telephone companies -- the Bell-licensed Cumberland Telephone and the independent Home Telephone Company. More than 75 percent of the large businesses and 9 percent of homes in Louisville subscribed to both services. *See* Milton L. Mueller, Jr., *Universal Service: Competition, Interconnection, and Monopoly in the Making of the American Telephone System,* (MIT Press and AEI Press, 1997) at 83.

[107] For instance, the 1913 Kingsbury Commitment, in which AT&T agreed to interconnect with independent local firms to provide long distance services, was made in response to a threatened antitrust suit, rather than calls to enable universal access for customers. *See supra* at n. 38.

products to be compatible with the products of another firm. Another factor leading to compatibility is that firms in nascent industries have an incentive to cooperate on setting common standards that will enable the industry to grow, so that later they can compete with one another over larger slices of the growing pie.[108]

In some cases, notably the personal computer market, more than one standard emerges. This result has nevertheless been influenced by consumer demand, as Apple is widely seen as meeting the demands of a niche market, while the IBM (Intel/Windows) standard meets the more general needs of the mass market. It is worth noting here that it has been Internet protocols and applications, such as Web browsers and the Java language, that have served to meet the demands of users of IBM and Apple's respective platforms to interact seamlessly with one another.[109] A final example of a standard emerging as a result of marketplace forces is the Internet itself. The protocols at the heart of the Internet, TCP/IP, only relatively recently became the dominant standard for networking, at the expense of a number of proprietary and non-proprietary standards including SNA, DecNet, and X.25.[110]

Although the marketplace is remarkably successful at generating compatible standards, it would be a mistake to conclude that this process is costless for consumers or firms. Purchasers of Sony's Betamax VCRs found it impossible to rent or buy movies after the VHS standard won the standards battle, while Sony was forced to concede and begin selling its competitors' standard. The fax machine market was very slow to mature without a fixed standard, delaying the widespread adoption of a product that soon came to be regarded as almost indispensable for both consumers and firms. In each case, the government could theoretically have chosen a standard, thereby avoiding these costs. Nevertheless, in the United States, consumers and firms rarely, if ever, call for government intervention in these cases.

The marketplace is the preferred means for setting compatible standards in most industries and for most products for a variety of reasons. First, an open marketplace for standards leads to healthy competition for the rewards of owning a standard, and often "second-mover" standards are able to overcome an industry leader by embodying their standards in better products, or more creative marketing of these products. For instance, VHS was able to overcome the Betamax lead to become the industry standard by providing longer recording times, among other things.[111] Second, as described above, innovators such as Apple Computer may target new products at niche markets, with consumers benefiting from the resulting variety. Such variety and innovation may not occur if a standard is chosen by non-market means. Therefore, while the marketplace may increase short-run costs involved with adopting new standards, the long-run marketplace benefits of competition and innovation are likely to more than make up for any short-run costs.

---

[108]   *See* Adam M. Brandenburger and Barry J. Nalebuff, *Co-opetition* (Doubleday, 1996).

[109]   *See infra at* n. 110.

[110]   Transmission Control Protocol (TCP) and Internet Protocol (IP) together form a "networking protocol that provides communication across interconnected networks, between computers with diverse hardware architectures and various operating systems." *Newton's* at 708.

[111]   Indeed, some attribute the initial advantage of VHS in the United States to the decision by its manufacturer to make tapes long enough to record a full American football game.

The marketplace should provide solutions to many, if not all, of the challenges that arise in the provision of current and new Internet services. Consumers, with expectations of universal connectivity and basic compatibility, are likely to demand that backbones essentially set standards for the provision of QoS services by agreeing to interconnect to provide these services. Backbones, in turn, may see that it is in their interest to interconnect in order to enable the market for QoS services to grow. If firms limit offerings of new QoS services to their own customers, other marketplace solutions are available that may ensure that consumers can remain connected to the full Internet. For instance, if two backbones are unable to coordinate an interconnection agreement enabling interconnection for QoS services, consumers may simply interconnect to more than one backbone, a practice known as multihoming, or turn to firms such as InterNAP that connect with all major backbones, enabling their customers to communicate directly with the customers of all major backbones without themselves multihoming. Marketplace demands and market-driven innovations may alleviate the costs of any Internet balkanization, if not preventing it altogether, in more efficient ways than would the imposition of any interconnection regulations on the Internet.

In summary, this paper argues that if one or more backbones choose not to interconnect with other backbones for the provision of new services in the future, this is likely to be a temporary phase. This phase would end as a result of market forces that would induce backbones to interconnect, while at the same time innovative firms might step into the breach to provide interconnection services for end users. Nevertheless, during this phase there may be calls to implement some form of interconnection regulation. The paper has argued above that such intervention would be relatively unique, as there is little precedent for the regulation of networks such as the Internet where there are low entry barriers on the cost-side. In addition, regulatory intervention would be a notable shift in United States policy.[112] As a result, any calls to intervene in the Internet market would require a correspondingly high burden of proof.

This paper attempts to inform any future discussion calling for regulatory intervention in the interactions between backbones. An affirmative case for regulatory intervention should include the following arguments. First, an argument may be made that the lack of interconnection would lead to market power, with adverse effects on consumers.[113] This argument should be accompanied by a showing that an ongoing regulatory approach, rather than an antitrust approach, is the appropriate solution to protect consumers from any potential adverse effects of market power. A second argument may be that, regardless of whether market power develops, interconnection between Internet backbones, enabling seamless communication between all Internet users, is in the public interest. In this case, a showing should be made that both identifies the benefits and the costs of mandating interconnection, and shows that the

---

[112] The 1996 Act states that it is the policy of the United States to "preserve the vibrant and competitive free market that presently exists for interactive computer services, unfettered by Federal or State regulation." 47 U.S.C. § 230 (b)(2).

[113] It is often argued that in markets with network externalities, lack of interconnection or compatibility will lead to "tipping," as consumers quickly converge on one standard in order to enjoy the benefits of being compatible with the largest possible installed base of the product. According to a recent book, "tipping occurs when a product subject to increasing returns [network externalities] generates sufficient momentum in market share that its domination of the market becomes inevitable." Stan J. Liebowitz and Stephen E. Margolis, *Winners, Losers & Microsoft: Competition and Antitrust in High Technology* (The Independent Institute, 1999) at 138. After studying a number of software markets in which Microsoft participates, the authors conclude that there is no evidence of tipping in these markets. *Id.*, at 228-229.

benefits outweigh the costs. The benefits stem from the network externalities that backbones will be able to deliver to end user customers; the costs of mandated interconnection could include a lowered incentive to innovate in providing new services, less variety of new services, and any regulatory costs incurred by firms and the regulatory agency. Finally, the realities of mandated interconnection would need to be addressed – who determines the terms of interconnection, the principles governing these terms of interconnection, and how these terms should be enforced. Given the complicated nature of interactions between backbones, intervention may be complex; however, as described above, it is likely to be unnecessary, as long as competition governs the interactions between backbones.

IV. International Interconnection Issues

In recent years, some non-U.S. carriers, largely from the Asia Pacific region, have complained that current international interconnection arrangements for the exchange of Internet traffic are not fair. The cost of international transmission capacity used for Internet traffic is typically not shared between carriers or backbones in connected countries; rather, one carrier generally pays for the entire circuit. The non-U.S. carriers claim that since traffic flows from international points to the United States are increasing, it is unfair that they pay for the entire circuit connecting their networks to the United States. These carriers propose that, as with international voice circuits, the cost should be shared between carriers at both ends. The question that this paper addresses is whether the interconnection agreements to which these carriers object are the result of competitive market forces, or whether there is a market failure that enables the U.S. backbones to impose unfair or anti-competitive interconnection agreements on the carriers outside of the United States.

A. Principles of International Telecommunications Regulation

International interconnection arrangements for telephony arose from the practicalities of interconnecting domestic telecommunications monopolies for international calling.[114] Until recently, domestic telecommunications monopolies could not enter foreign markets to terminate traffic, nor could they turn to competitors as an alternative to the incumbent carrier in a country.[115] As a result, completion of an international call needed to be jointly undertaken by the domestic monopolies at the originating and terminating ends. An arrangement emerged in which each carrier provides half the transmission circuit needed to route calls from one country to the other. In addition, the international accounting rate system provides a framework in which the originating carrier that bills customers for international calls compensates the carrier in the called country for terminating calls.[116] It is worth noting for the present discussion that, as competition

---

[114]   *See* Henry Ergas and Paul Paterson, "International Telecommunications Settlement Arrangements; An Unsustainable Inheritance?," *Telecommunications Policy*, February 1991, at 29-41.

[115]   Countries representing over 90 percent of global telecommunications revenues committed to remove barriers to foreign participation in domestic telecommunications markets by signing the World Trade Organization (WTO) Agreement on Basic Telecommunications Services that took effect in 1998. For more information on the WTO Agreement on Basic Telecommunications Services, see the WTO Web site at http://www.wto.org/wto/services.

[116]   The accounting rate is meant to represent the total cost of completing an international call. The originating carrier compensates the terminating carrier based on the settlement rate, which is usually one half of the accounting rate.

increasingly emerges in countries on both sides of international circuits, commercial negotiations between carriers are beginning to supplant these legacy international regulations.

The Internet has not been subject to these legacy international regulations. Instead, the Internet runs over leased or privately owned lines that are not subject to the accounting rate system as long as they are not used to provide public telecommunications services.[117] In addition, there are no provisions for sharing the cost of these leased or privately owned lines between countries. As a result, according to a OECD report, entitled *Internet Traffic Exchange: Developments and Policy*, "the Internet model for financing international infrastructure ... effectively shifts the financial mid-point for traffic exchange from oceans (as in the case of cables) and geostationary orbit (as in the case of satellites) to Internet exchange points [such as NAPs]."[118] There are no guidelines, however, for determining the location of the Internet exchange point where two backbones will meet to exchange traffic, instead, the meet point results from private negotiations between the backbones. Some carriers, particularly from the Asia-Pacific region, have questioned whether the results of these negotiations are fair.

B. International Cost-Sharing Issue

1. Background

In recent years, a number of non-U.S. carriers have objected to the interconnection agreements governing the flows of Internet traffic between international points and the United States.[119] Telstra, an Australian domestic and international carrier, has claimed that "to access U.S.-based Internet sites ... U.S. carriers have insisted that foreign carriers pay for both of the required international half-circuits, i.e., for 100% of the cost of the international link."[120] Telstra claims that roughly 30 percent of Internet traffic flowing between the United States and Australia is flowing from Australia to the United States, "due mainly to U.S. Internet users increasingly drawing on Australian Internet content."[121] Because Telstra pays for the entire link between Australia and the United States, Telstra claims it is effectively subsidizing U.S. carriers and U.S. ISPs whose customers are accessing Australian content. In 1999, Telstra estimated that "Australian ISPs will incur costs of around $175 million to support provision of internet services by US ISPs to their US customers."[122] Telstra also argued that the current pricing arrangements

---

[117] For more information on the distinction between public telecommunications services and private networks such as the Internet, *see* OECD Report at 35-36.

[118] *Id.* at 36.

[119] *See* J. Scott Marcus, *Designing Wide Area Networks*, at 285-286.

[120] Telstra compares these arrangements with traditional telephony arrangements: "[i]n contrast, where international telephone service is involved, the U.S. and foreign carrier each pay for their own half-circuit." Telstra Corporation Comments (filed Feb. 4, 1997 in IB Docket No. 96-261, *In the Matter of International Settlement Rates*)(Telstra ISR Comments) at 3. *See also* Telstra Corporation Reply Comments (filed Mar. 31, 1997 in IB Docket No. 96-261, *In the Matter of International Settlement Rates*)(Telstra ISR Reply Comments) at 4-5; Telstra Corporation Comments (filed Jan. 5, 1998 in CC Docket No. 97-211, *Applications of WorldCom, Inc. and MCI Communications Corporation for Transfer of Control of MCI Communications Corporation to WorldCom, Inc*)(Telstra MCI/WorldCom Comments) at 8.

[121] Telstra ISR Comments at 3.

[122] Telstra Press Release, "Why are Australians Paying More than They Should for Internet Access to the USA?" November 30, 1999. A general disclaimer on Telstra's web site notes that this information is no longer current, and is provided for historical purposes only. *See* http://www.telstra.com.au.

"appear to be unjust and unreasonable in violation of Section 201(b) of the Communications Act."[123] Similarly, in January of 1999, a number of other Asia-Pacific carriers sent a letter on this subject to a number of U.S. backbone providers, and business, government, and Internet organizations,[124] in which they claim that "the increasing demand for information from the [Asia-Pacific] region and the bi-directional traffic make the [ISPs] in the US in effect free-riding on the circuits and gateways/ports provided by the [Asia-Pacific] region ISPs."[125]

As a remedy to their perceived problems with the current system, Telstra proposes that "under an equitable regime the cost-allocation of Internet capacity must reflect the traffic flows."[126] Similarly, in their letter, the Asia-Pacific carriers requested that U.S. backbones "share the cost of international Internet backbone between the US and the AP region according to their usage or benefits" and urge a study of the "actual traffic as the basis of usage-based or cost-oriented charging and settlement arrangements."[127]

A couple of international organizations are currently studying the international Internet cost-sharing issue raised by the non-U.S. carriers. The Asia Pacific Economic Cooperation (APEC) forum has raised this issue, under the rubric of international charging arrangements for Internet services (ICAIS), in 1998 at a Ministerial meeting on the Telecommunications and Information industry in Singapore. The Ministerial Declaration called for "the study, and, if and when appropriate, development, by the next APEC Ministerial Meeting on Telecommunications and Information Industry, of compatible and sustainable international charging arrangements for Internet services...."[128] The Terms of Reference for this study solicited, "[i]f and when appropriate, and based on the findings of the study, proposals on the kinds of market and cost-based commercial and/or regulatory responses necessary to create more compatible and sustainable international charging arrangements for Internet services to promote the further development of and access to the Asia-Pacific Information Infrastructure (APII)."[129] The United States, in a background paper to the APEC Telecommunications Working Group, maintained that "there is no need for government intervention into relationships between Internet Service Providers."[130] The United States further contended that "cost efficient arrangements for Internet

[123] Section 201(b) states in part that "all charges, practices, classifications, and regulations for and in connection with [interstate or foreign communication by wire or radio], shall be just and reasonable...." U.S.C. § 201(b). Telstra MCI/WorldCom Comments at 8.

[124] "Statement on the Cost Sharing of the International Internet Interconnection Link between the U.S.A. and Asia-Pacific Region," signed by representatives of The Communications Authority of Thailand, Chunghwa Telecom (Taiwan), Indonesia Satellite Corp., KDD Corp. (Japan), Korea Telecom, Philippines Long Distance Telephone Company, Singapore Telecommunications Ltd., and Telekom Malaysia Berhad (Jan. 26, 1999)(Asia-Pacific Carrier Letter). *See also* Newsbytes News Network, "Asian Carriers Protest High Internet Connection Charges," (Jan. 27, 1999)(Newsbytes Jan. 27 Article).

[125] Asia-Pacific Carrier Letter at 2.

[126] Telstra ISR Comments at 4.

[127] *Id.*

[128] *The Singapore Declaration* of the Third APEC Ministerial Meeting on the Telecommunications and Information Industry, 3-5 June 1998, Singapore, http://www.apii.or kr/telwg/ICAIS/singapore html, at § 11.c.

[129] "A Study of Compatible and Sustainable International Charging Arrangements for Internet Services (ICAIS) Terms of Reference", http://www.apii.or kr/telwg/ICAIS/tor html, at § 2.e.

[130] U.S. Background Paper, "International Charging Arrangements for Internet Services (ICAIS)," submitted to APEC Telecommunications Working Group for discussion (Feb. 20, 1999)(U.S. ICAIS Background Paper), http://www.apii.or kr/telwg/19tel/plenary/plen-g-01.html. *See also* September 1999 Appendix to the U.S. ICAIS Background Paper.

traffic will continue to be worked out most quickly if the market is not hampered by government regulation."[131]

The ICAIS study commissioned by APEC was recently completed; while the authors discuss various Internet charging mechanisms, they do not make recommendations or express opinions about the imposition of such charging mechanisms.[132] However, they made several relevant findings. First, the authors found that "[t]rans-Pacific and intra-Asian capacity is more expensive and less competitive than is the case within North America, on trans-Atlantic routes, or within Europe."[133] Second, they found that "North American and other backbone carriers are expanding rapidly in the Asia-Pacific region."[134] Finally, they found that "the rapid deployment of new capacity will dramatically reduce the unit cost of international charges [for Internet services], irrespective of the structure of the charging arrangements."[135]

Based on the instructions adopted at the 1998 APEC Ministerial Meeting, the ICAIS issue was again on the agenda at the APEC Ministerial Meeting on Telecommunications in Cancun, Mexico from May 24-26, 2000. At this meeting, the Ministers reaffirmed "the importance of mutually beneficial arrangements on [ICAIS], to allow a continued expansion of the Asia Pacific Information Infrastructure."[136] The Cancun Ministerial Declaration stated that "Governments need not intervene in private business agreements on International Charging Agreements for Internet Services achieved in a competitive environment, but where there are dominant players or de facto monopolies, governments must play a role in promoting fair competition."[137] However, the Programme of Action resulting from the Ministerial notes that the APEC Telecommunications Working Group (TEL) should continue to discuss charging arrangements, noting that these arrangements should account for traffic flow patterns.[138]

Several reports on this issue have not supported any active government role in regulating international interconnection arrangements. The Organization for Economic Co-operation and Development (OECD) argued that "[a]t this stage, the best way forward is for industry to initiate discussion on the financing of Internet traffic exchange, for example, via the Asia-Pacific Internet Association's call for comments and other industry forums. The role of government is to stay abreast of these discussions and support industry-led solutions."[139] In December 1999,

---

[131]   *Id.*

[132]   James Savage, Robert Frieden, and Timothy Denton, *ICAIS Module 3 Final Report,* April 2000 (*ICAIS Module 3*), at 3-4. *See* http://www.tmdenton.com.

[133]   *Id.* at 9.

[134]   *Id.* at 10.

[135]   *Id.* at 11.

[136]   The Fourth APEC Ministerial Meeting of the Telecommunications and Information Industry (TELMIN4), *Press Conference.*

[137]   TELMIN4, *Cancun Declaration*, May 24-26, 2000 at Annex B.

[138]   *See id.*, Annex A, APEC Telecommunications Working Group (TEL), *Programme of Action*, ("the TEL should continue to discuss the international development of the Internet, including charging arrangements, noting the initial suggestions in the proposals made by the ICAIS Task Force that: 1. Where measurement tools are available and acceptable, charging arrangements should be based on traffic flow patterns for each type of service, taking into account which side has generated the traffic. 2. In the absence of efficient measurement tools, charging arrangements for international links should be based on the ration of inbound to outbound traffic flow.").

[139]   *See* OECD Report at 35-44. The Asia Pacific Internet Association issued a call for papers on the ICAIS topic. "Calls for Papers (CFP) International Internet Infrastructure: Inequities or reality, is there a problem with trans-oceanic Internet backbone infrastructure financing?" Sept. 24, 1997, http://www.apia.org.

the International Telecommunications Union (ITU) Telecommunications Sector Study Group 3 (ITU-T/SG3) issued a report arguing that "the PSTN costing model is inappropriate for the Internet," but the group was otherwise "unable to develop an agreed set of principles on the equitable cost compensation between circuit providers."[140]

The first step towards changing the international Internet charging arrangement status quo came from the ITU-T/SG3 during a meeting in Geneva that concluded on April 18, 2000.[141] The study group adopted a proposal, raised by the Asia and Oceania Region tariff group, recommending that "administrations involved in the provision of international Internet connection negotiate and agree bilateral commercial arrangements applying to direct international Internet connections whereby each administration will be compensated for the cost that it incurs in carrying traffic that is generated by the other administration."[142] This draft recommendation will be submitted to the ITU World Telecommunications Standardization Assembly (WTSA) for approval. The WTSA meets in Montreal in September 2000. The recommendation did not explain its departure from contrary conclusions that emerged after two years of study by a rapporteur's group established by Study Group 3 itself. The United States has submitted to the WTSA meeting formal contributions in opposition to both the substance of this recommendation and the procedures used in its adoption.

2. Analysis

It is important to note at the outset that there is no discrimination against non-U.S. carriers in interconnection arrangements. U.S. Internet backbones treat domestic and foreign backbones the same when negotiating the meet point for Internet exchange. In response to Telstra's specific claims raised above, in the *MCI/WorldCom Order*, the Commission did not agree that the merging backbones' practices violated section 201(b) of the Communications Act. The Commission found that "the record does not demonstrate that WorldCom or MCI provides services subject to Title II regulation on rates, terms, and conditions that are unjust or unreasonably discriminatory, in violation of the Communications Act."[143] No indication has been provided by the Asia-Pacific carriers that prove that the interconnection agreements to which they object reflect anti-competitive actions on the part of U.S. backbones.

The Asia-Pacific carriers base their objection to current interconnection agreements on the relative flow of traffic between the United States and international points; however, traffic flows are not a good indicator of the relative benefits of an Internet interconnection between backbones, and therefore provide a poor basis for allocating any costs. First, unlike a phone call, it is impossible to determine who originally initiated any given transmission on the Internet. For instance, a packet flowing from the United States to Japan either may be part of a transmission such as an email that was initiated by a user in the United States, or part of a Web page being sent in response to a request initiated by a user in Japan. It is therefore not clear who should pay

---

[140]   Study Group 3, International Telecommunications Union, "Final Report for Internet Rapporteurs Group," COM 3-77-E, October 1999, a report adopted by the Study Group in December 1999.
[141]   *See Communications Daily*, "ITU Study Group Recommends Settlement Rate System for Internet," April 24, 2000 (April 24 *Comm Daily*).
[142]   Five countries, the United States, Canada, the United Kingdom, Holland, and Russia, opposed this recommendation. *Id.*
[143]   *MCI/WorldCom Order*, 13 FCC Rcd at 18117, para. 159.

for the cost of transmitting a given traffic flow from the United States to Japan. In addition, if a transmission is a Web page, it is not clear who received more benefits from the transmission – the customer that requested the Web page or the content provider that supplied the information. In fact, both benefit from the ability to use the Internet to initiate cross-border transactions that may never have occurred but for the Internet.[144]

In the specific case raised by the Asia-Pacific carriers, it is also difficult to assign benefits or costs from Internet interconnections based on traffic flows because the United States acts as a hub for Asia-Pacific intra-regional traffic.[145] Thus, some of the traffic flowing to the United States from the Asia-Pacific region may immediately return to another part of the Asia-Pacific region; this traffic does not represent a benefit for which customers of United States backbones should pay any share. In sum, it is not possible to determine the value of an Internet connection between the United States and the Asia-Pacific region or elsewhere based solely on the Internet traffic flows between these regions.

The Asia-Pacific carriers have argued that, based on their equation of traffic flows to benefits, U.S. backbones should share the cost of the transmission capacity between the Asia-Pacific region and the United States, a system that would essentially impose legacy international regulations on the Internet.[146] The Internet is a worldwide network, however, whose value cannot be split over only one section of transmission capacity. For example, while a backbone in the Asia-Pacific region may provide the transmission capacity to connect with a backbone provider at one point in the United States, it may thereby receive access to the latter backbone's extensive national network within the United States, and increasingly to the backbone's investments in connections to Europe and other parts of the world. It is difficult therefore to conclude that there is a net subsidy going from the customers of the Asia-Pacific backbone to those of the U.S. backbone.[147]

The meet point for Internet exchange is determined as a result of commercial negotiations that take into account more than just traffic flows between two networks.[148] Traffic flows on the Internet do not necessarily provide a good indication of the benefits of an Internet interconnection. In addition, as discussed above, backbones negotiating an interconnection

---

[144] The same is often true for a telephone call that may lead to a transaction that benefits both parties. However, in telephony, explicit mechanisms exist for either the calling party or the called party to pay for a particular call. In general, the calling party pays, but the calling party may place a collect call, which the called party can either accept or refuse, or the called party can pay in advance for all incoming calls by providing a toll-free 800 number. These mechanisms do not currently exist on the Internet, and therefore a system in which either a sender or receiver of information pays for a transmission based solely on net traffic flows may not be optimal.

[145] *See, e.g.,* Newsbytes Jan. 27 Article. ("The Internet infrastructure in Asia at present only allows a small percentage of regional traffic to stay within Asia. [This] forces much [traffic] to the United States, which acts as a common interconnection point for Asia."). *See also* OECD Report at 37-38.

[146] Indeed, according to Peter Coroneos, Executive Director of the Internet Industry Association of Australia (IIA), "this bilateral pricing arrangement [applying to voice traffic] should logically also apply to data markets." Newsbytes News Network, "Australian Net Industry To Join Asian Net Links Protest," Jan. 29, 1999 (Newsbytes Jan. 29 Article). Mr. Coroneos stated that "[t]he fact that data is not similarly priced [as voice] is more of a historical accident than a creature of design. If we were to develop a pricing model from scratch today, I would be amazed if a degree of reciprocity were not provided for, notwithstanding the imbalance in bargaining power." *Id.*

[147] *See also* OECD Report at 39.

[148] *See also id.* at 40.

arrangement consider, among other things, relative infrastructure investments as well as the composition and location of customers and content providers. According to all publicly available information, there is therefore no indication that any U.S. backbones are exercising market power with respect to non-U.S. carriers. Legacy international regulations should therefore not be imposed on backbones.

C. Marketplace Solutions

As with domestic interconnection arrangements, backbone providers negotiate international interconnection terms in a competitive environment, and base their decisions on whether, how, and where to interconnect by weighing the benefits and costs of such interconnection. As the Internet industry evolves in the United States and abroad, competitive market forces continue to influence the nature of interconnection agreements between U.S. and foreign backbone providers. As shown in Figure 12, the number of Internet users outside the United States has been growing faster than the number of users within the United States, and, the number of users in the rest of the world now exceeds that in the United States. In the long term, this growth may have two effects on Internet cost-sharing arrangements. First, the amount of content available in the rest of the world is likely to increase to meet this increased demand, providing foreign backbone providers with more content, resulting in more leverage for interconnection negotiations with U.S. backbones. Indeed, there are reports that at least one Asian company, Internet Initiative Japan Inc., already connects with U.S. backbones on an equal basis owing to the large amount of content that it aggregates from Japanese companies and ISPs.[149] Second, U.S. backbones are responding to the increased demand in the rest of the world by investing in both international transmission capacity and networks in other countries. For instance, Level 3 has invested in capacity to Europe and within Europe, and is part of a consortium building transmission capacity to Japan.[150] U.S. backbones that have invested in international transmission capacity can then exchange traffic with foreign backbones directly in the foreign country, increasing the options available to foreign backbones that do not wish to pay for transmission capacity to exchange traffic with U.S. backbones in the United States.[151]

Other market-based solutions may further reduce the transport costs incurred by Asia-Pacific carriers.[152] As with domestic backbones seeking to reduce traffic flows and alleviate congestion, backbones outside the United States can use caching and mirror sites to reduce the amount of traffic flowing from the United States to international points and thereby reduce the need for transmission capacity. Additionally, increased competition within the Asia-Pacific region will lower the cost of leased lines between countries in the Asia-Pacific region, enabling more direct intra-regional Internet traffic exchange and correspondingly reducing the costs associated with using the United States as a hub for this purpose.[153] Telegeography recently noted that "in Europe, where telecom liberalization has been the greatest and country-to-country

---

[149]   Newsbytes Jan. 27 Article.

[150]   Boardwatch Magazine's Directory of Internet Service Providers, 11th Edition, 1999, at 130-133. *See also* OECD Report at 40; U.S. ICAIS Background Paper at para. 33.

[151]   *See ICAIS Module 3* at 9, 10.

[152]   *See also* OECD Report at 40-41; September 1999 Appendix to U.S. ICAIS Background Paper ("Alternative peering arrangements between ISPs are being developed.").

[153]   *See also* U.S. ICAIS Background Paper at para. 22; *ICAIS Module 3* at 10.

bandwidth prices have dropped the fastest, two thirds of international Internet connectivity remains in-region." The explanation is that "the move away from a U.S.-centric architecture depends on well-developed local infrastructure, and a regulatory environment which neither prohibits connectivity nor prices it out of reach."[154]

Finally, another market-based solution is suggested by Peter Coroneos, the Director of the Internet Industry Association of Australia. Complaining about the practices of U.S. backbones, he argues that "you can only have the market upset for a period of time before they start looking for ways to avoid the pain." As a result, "alternative solutions will emerge which will leave those currently acting monopolistically with a diminishing market share."[155] As discussed earlier in this paper, it is exactly the presence of alternatives for backbones seeking interconnection that prevents monopolistic actions by other backbones. To the extent that the carriers outside the United States find alternatives to the U.S. backbones, these U.S. backbones are likely to respond to this reduced demand by providing cost-sharing arrangements that the non-U.S. carriers find acceptable. Such competitive pressures and responses are the hallmark of competition in the Internet industry and make any international regulation for Internet interconnection unnecessary.

V. Conclusion

In the past several years, a number of Internet backbones, in the United States and abroad, have questioned whether the commercial interconnection negotiations between backbone providers can yield fair outcomes for all parties. In addition, backbones may attempt in the future to differentiate themselves from their competitors by not interconnecting to provide certain new services. As a result, there may increasingly be calls to impose domestic and/or international interconnection obligations on Internet backbone providers. The paper shows how the market outcomes of a competitive Internet backbone market can differ from the network industries characterized by market power that historically warranted interconnection regulations. In addition, antitrust and competition protections can prevent any anti-competitive consolidation among Internet backbone providers. In sum, this paper argues that any traditional telecommunications regulation of Internet backbone interconnection is made unnecessary by a competitive backbone market, a conclusion that is consistent with section 230 of the 1996 Act.[156] The paper recognizes that future circumstances may arise that lead parties to renew calls to impose industry-specific regulations on the Internet backbone market, and argues that these parties bear the burden of identifying the anti-competitive harms that would be remedied, as well as identifying the best means for resolving these harms.

---

[154]   *See* http://www.telegeography.com.
[155]   Newsbytes Jan. 29 Article.
[156]   *See supra* n. 62.

Figure 1: Peering

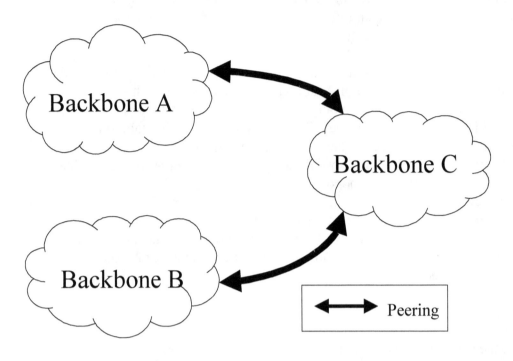

Figure 2: Network Access Point

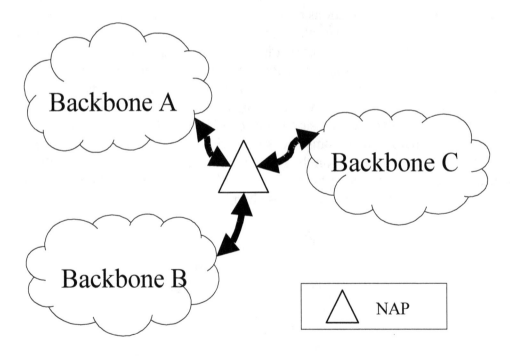

Figure 3: Private Peering

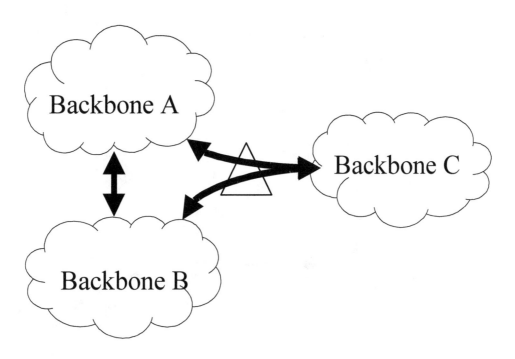

Figure 4: Transit

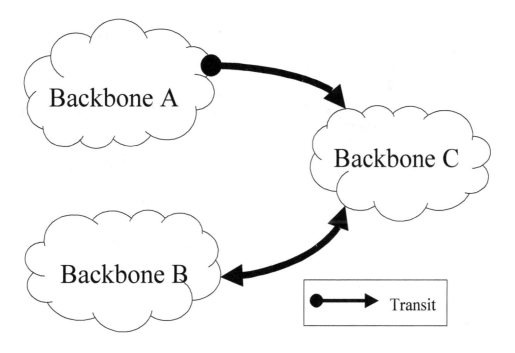

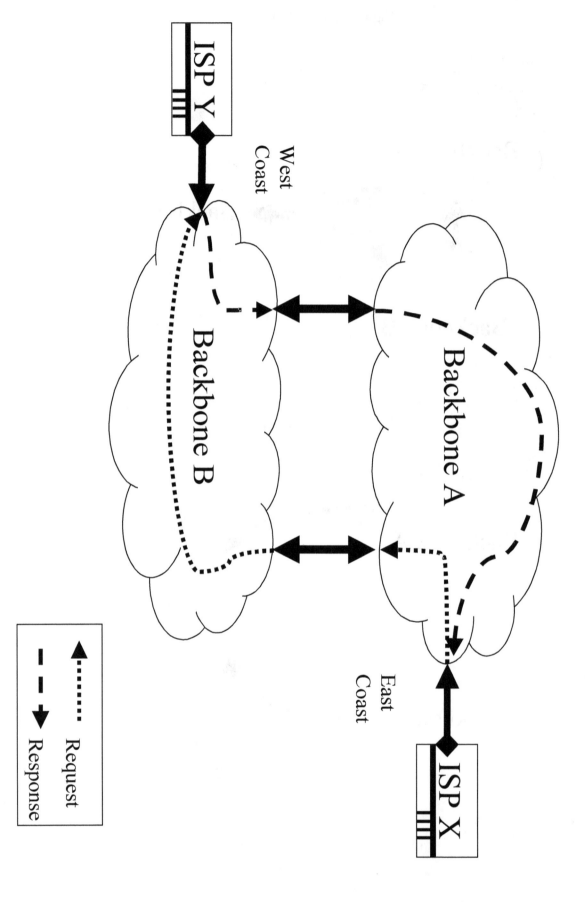

Figure 5: Hot-Potato Routing

42

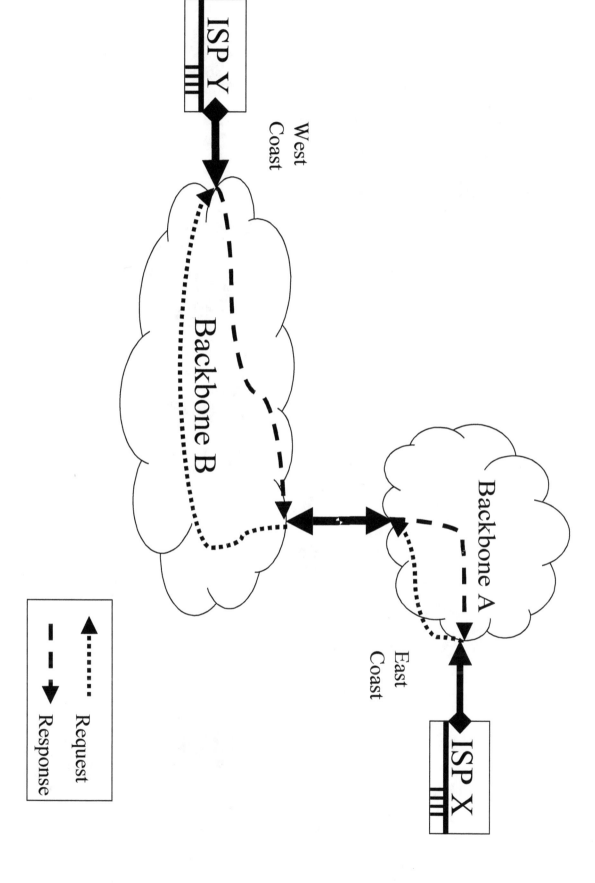

Figure 6: Example of Free Riding

West
Coast

Backbone B

Backbone A

East
Coast

ISP Y

ISP X

Request

Response